GETTING
MORE DONE
IN *Less* TIME...

& HAVING
MORE FUN
DOING IT!

GETTING MORE DONE IN Less TIME...
& HAVING MORE FUN DOING IT!

MIKE PHILLIPS

BETHANY HOUSE PUBLISHERS
MINNEAPOLIS, MINNESOTA 55438
A Division of Bethany Fellowship, Inc.

Published by Bethany House Publishers
A Division of Bethany Fellowship, Inc.
6820 Auto Club Road, Minneapolis, Minnesota 55438

Printed in the United States of America

Phillips, Mike, 1946-
    Getting more done in less time—and having
more fun doing it!

    1. Success.   I. Title.
HF5386.P585   640'.43   82-1245
ISBN 0-87123-198-0 (pbk.)   AACR2

To Michael McClure

A friend,
an invaluable co-worker,
and a man of God

OTHER BOOKS BY THE SAME AUTHOR:

Building Respect, Responsibility and Spiritual Values in Your Child
A Christian Family in Action
A Survival Guide for Tough Times
Growth of a Vision
Does Christianity Make Sense?
Blueprint for Raising a Child
Control Through Planned Budgeting—A Management Guide for Christian Bookstores
A Vision for the Church

ABOUT THE AUTHOR

MIKE PHILLIPS was raised in California, graduated from Humboldt State University, and had every intention of pursuing a career in physics or mathematics. But instead he began selling and writing books. Beginning with a part-time selling effort twelve years ago, today Mike is General Manager of One Way, Ltd., and a chain of west-coast Christian bookstores. He and his wife Judy have three sons.

CONTENTS

Part I

YOU CAN GET MORE DONE!

1. "THERE'S TOO MUCH TO DO AND THE DAY'S NOT LONG ENOUGH!"

"I just don't have time! There are books I haven't read, projects around the house I need to start, places I want to take my children, letters I should write, people I should visit. . . .

"And that's not to mention my job (you should see my desk! It's piled high with work), the committee at church, and PTA responsibilities.

"There just isn't enough time to get everything done!"

Sound familiar? If you're normal I'm sure it does. There are so many things you would like to do and need to do—good things, important things. Yet your life is already full. Your days are consumed simply keeping your head above water with your present obligations. You live from one "Things to Do" list to another, adding two items on the bottom for every one you check off the top.

It's a normal predicament. We're all victims. The active person with a wide range of interests always has more to do than he or she can realistically hope to accomplish. And it's frustrating!

That's what this book is all about. You will learn to get your *whole* list done—the things on the top *and* the things on the bottom. Not only will you learn to get them done, but you will learn to forge into new areas that need your time and attention.

But you're not going to train yourself to move faster, and frantically cram fourteen hours worth of activities into eight hours. Such a pace might get items crossed off your list, but it would also wear you out. Instead, we're going to examine an altogether different approach. We'll explore principles usually reserved for management textbooks which tell executives how to accelerate their climb up the corporate ladder. We'll even occasionally throw in a bit of "management" terminology. However, you'll discover that these same principles can be applied in very practical and exciting ways by *everyone*—the leader and executive, as well as the housewife, student, secretary, laborer, committee member, and salesperson. You'll discover *how to get more done, in less time, with greater efficiency and less frustration.*

That may sound like an ambitious goal. And there was a time in my life when I would have considered it an impossibility. I, as well as my wife, faced insurmountable "lists" and was constantly pulled in many directions at once by time demands. I was continually frustrated. Had you known me then you would undoubtedly have said to yourself, "If there's anyone whose time-use habits I *don't* want to imitate, he's the guy!"

But my wife and I have made some very practical discoveries that now enable us to get more done in less time. We've had to make changes to keep pace with the Lord's work in our lives. I am a businessman in charge of a corporation, which includes several stores spread over 600 miles, a publishing arm, and other aspects. My wife is involved in the business as a bookkeeper and faces a demanding workload. We both teach, in our church and other churches. We are often involved in family counseling. We have three young and very active boys with severe allergies and learning disabilities. This has meant hundreds of hours of research, long trips to various specialists, and the formulation of an in-home teaching curriculum to meet their needs. In addition we both have numerous outside relationships, interests, and responsibilities. We are *busy* people. Daily we encounter more work than we could ever complete apart from *a high degree of productivity.*

But in the midst of the pressures and frustrations of quarterly tax reports, customer complaints, church problems, home remodeling, tonsilitis, double hernias, adenoidectomies, salesmen, headaches, bank loans, allergy-related learning disabilities, hiring and firing, IRS audits, bounced checks, lease negotiations, and the unceasing needs of young children, we have made breakthroughs that make a significant difference in every chaotic and demanding day.

Because of these similarities between our lives and your own, the solutions we offer you do not come from some world far removed from yours. The application of these ideas has originated in our own hectic daily schedule. We had to *learn* to get organized (and believe me, it wasn't easy!). We had to *learn* to be efficient—just to survive. We had to *learn* to spend our time more wisely. Therefore, these principles will be useful to *you* in whatever situation you are in.

In whatever ways the specifics of our individual lives fall together, we *all* share one thing in common—we want to get more done with the time, talents, and resources we have. *We want to live up to our potential.*

That involves learning to *manage* our time, activities, families, organizations, talents, other people—and ourselves! Every productive person is a manager. *Management is not a profession; it is the means to a fulfilling life.*

Perhaps the most useful parts of this book will be the questions at the end of each chapter and the worksheets at the end of the book. You desire to discover practical ways to increase your efficiencey. The questions and worksheets could well provide the key.

The questions will bring you face-to-face with your own inefficiencies. Self-analysis is never easy, but remember, this book is designed to point you in a productive new direction. It cannot succeed unless you make a certain investment. The point is to evaluate yourself thoroughly and honestly so that you can clearly picture your particular needs. Work through the book slowly. Make sure your answers are *complete*—this is an "essay test." There are no right and wrong answers. You are on the right track if you have confronted yourself in humble honesty.

If you are using this book with a group, the questions provide an ideal springboard to discussion. If you are studying this book as a married couple, the questions and worksheets will help you discover what you want to accomplish and become as husband and wife.

Even if it takes you six months to plow through this book, you will learn the art of effective goal-setting and planning. The results will be worth the effort! You will be filled with purpose and direction and will be on the way toward accomplishing those goals you have decided to reach.

You can read motivational books, listen to motivational tapes, and attend motivational seminars. But often you will be left stranded, without practical direction—what to do today and tomorrow. Because I have been in your position (even still am in many ways), I intend this book to be different. When you finish this book, you *will* know what to do—TODAY!

Learning to manage your time will require thought and effort. I won't try to kid you into thinking it's going to be easy! Therefore, don't allow mental laziness to keep you from what could be one of the most significant experiences of your life. Pick up a pencil and use it! Make this a *work*-book, not simply a book you read once and forever file on the bookshelf. Read, re-read, underline, jot down questions, design your own applications, write me a letter if need be.

But whatever you do, *apply the principles*. Make them work! If you do, I guarantee productive accomplishment to be within YOUR reach!

Evaluate Yourself

1. What are my most perplexing time frustrations?
2. What are some of the things which I want to do but just never have time for?
3. Do I gain a sense of permanent accomplishment from my activities? Or do I feel as if I'm only fulfilling my day-to-day necessities?

2. WANT TO ACCOMPLISH MORE? YOU CAN

Pat Coleman—The Frustrated Housewife

Pat has been married five years and has three young children. She is a conscientious mother and seems to be doing a good job.

But she sometimes wonders! Two of the three have terrible tantrums. It seems many days are nothing but screams, spankings, and fraught nerves. By day's end Pat often is worn out and has a headache.

Pat is a sensitive woman with a wide range of interests. She sings well, plays the piano, and once harbored a secret ambition to be a concert violinist. But that was long ago. Now Pat's life is the children, her husband's career, and the home. Basically, she is content and wouldn't trade her life for a "career." Yet Pat is tired and frustrated. Her many interests lie dormant, unable to find outward expression. She rarely plays the piano anymore and hasn't been asked for months to sing in church. She longingly thinks back to her single years when she was more involved in the church—singing in the choir, teaching a Sunday school class. She likes to sew but rarely has the opportunity. There are friends she never sees. She can't remember when she last had time to relax and read a book. Daily quiet time to meditate and recoup her energy seems an impossibility. She has forgotten what such a time even feels like.

Pat Coleman is a talented, well-rounded woman, frustrated by the one-dimensional nature of her life. There is much she'd like to have time for. She doesn't want out of her present responsibilities; she just longs for a broadened spectrum of expression, to retain her home life and yet fulfill herself in other areas.

Dave Jenkins—The Wheel-Spinning Visionary

Dave is the shift foreman in a tire manufacturing plant. He is intelligent, skilled and good at his job. He has advanced steadily over the years. However, though thoroughly competent, he is somehow not outstanding. He is never considered for promotion into the upper echelons of company management.

Dave recognizes he has reached a plateau. There may be one or two advancements available, but he sees a definite limit to where he can rise within the company. He has been at his foreman's position now for five years and is beginning to feel stagnant. He is in a rut.

Dave has always been full of good ideas and dreams. At one time he felt he had a chance to break into the pro football ranks (he was an outstanding college linebacker). He knows he has abilities that could really amount to something if he had the opportunity to express them. He has toyed secretly with the idea of returning to school to prepare for foreign mission work. If he had the initial money to invest, Dave knows he could be successful in real estate or in a small business. Under the right circumstances, he is certain some of his dreams could be realized. He longs to branch out, to be on his own, to succeed, to amount to something.

Yet, as Dave assesses his life, he has to admit that he is going nowhere. He is hopelessly stuck in his present job, not making enough to put away funds for investment, starting a business, or returning to school. He is aging, he's putting on weight and his hairline is receding. When Dave looks in the mirror each morning, all the deep frustrations of his unfulfilled life rush at him.

He recently read in the paper that one of his college

teammates (for whom everything *did* fall just right and who went on to become a moderately successful NFL running back) had been elected to the university hall of fame. *I could have made it,* Dave thinks to himself. *If it hadn't been for that ankle injury in the fourth game—well, who knows?* The lengthy article about his friend's glowing athletic career symbolized to Dave the contrast between his life and what he had once hoped it would be.

Dave Jenkins is caught in the frustration of mid-life mediocrity. Life seems to be passing him by and he seems powerless to alter that trend.

Pete and Cindy Higdon—The Activists

Pete and Cindy are in their early thirties. They have no children. They have no time for a family, for they are too deeply immersed in a variety of activities and interests.

Pete is the assistant pastor of a large church. His outgoing nature thrives on activity. He leads two weekly Bible studies and conducts a seminar twice monthly in guidance techniques for Christian schoolteachers. He is committed to a number of church-based ministries—a weekly prison service, a visitation program, a literature ministry, and an outreach training school. He also carries out the normal administrative aspects of his job. These include printing the weekly church newsletter, maintaining regular office hours, making weekly calls on sick members, leading the singing in the evening services, and serving on three committees and one board. Pete also co-leads the Junior High group and does all the planning for a quarterly men's leadership retreat.

In addition, Pete has personal commitments that demand his "free" time. He plays city-league softball during the summer, mans a booktable one afternoon each month at the local university, and is an avid spokesman on current issues at city council meetings. And there's the city-wide evangelistic crusade coming in seven months which he agreed to co-direct.

Pete is a genuine go-go boy—a man of action on every possible front!

His wife, Cindy, is much the same, though in different areas. She is a schoolteacher (which is a great help since Pete's active life has not brought in a steady income). Several school activities demand Cindy's time—the PTA (she is program chairman) and a committee responsible for interaction between the school district and the community; she is even considering running for the school board. As the assistant pastor's wife, Cindy attends a women's prayer meeting on Thursday nights and leads a women's Sunday school class. She attends all the regular services with Pete, serves on the board of deaconesses, and the Christian Education Committee. Each summer Cindy directs the church Bible school, conducts a leader's training session, and teaches the Primary class.

Pete and Cindy are enthusiastic, outgoing, eager and energetic. To be around them is to be left breathless. Walk into Pete's office and you have the immediate impression you are in the presence of a busy and important man—the desk is cluttered, the phone is ringing, his "in" and "out" boxes are stacked high with unanswered mail, his bookshelf is just sloppy enough to look well used, and Pete himself is a dynamo of activity.

Yet those closest to Pete and Cindy worry about them. They wonder how solid their marriage relationship is. The couple has obligations six nights a week and rarely slow down long enough to stop to talk to each other. For all the haste, there seems to be a degree of mismanaged flurry.

Does Pete's cluttered office demonstrate the importance of his involvements, or does it reveal inefficiency and disorder in his life? Are the endless activities a cover-up for unproductiveness? Are the endless meetings a clue that deep down, Pete and Cindy don't know what they really want to accomplish in life?

Barbard Redmond—Who Watches Too Many
Days Simply Dissolve

Barbara is mature and for the most part contented. She has no serious reservations about her station in life. She is forty-two. Her marriage is good. She has a number of satisfying friendships and a rewarding church life. To the outsider Barbara would appear to be living a fulfilling life.

Yet something inside her whispers that if she could just plug in to a more disciplined daily schedule, she could achieve some major things. For Barbara is largely disorganized and inefficient. Many days seem to just disappear, as if through a sieve.

Where do the days . . . the weeks . . . the years go? she wonders. *Do I read too much? Do I spend too many afternoons window shopping or puttering in the yard? Do I watch too much TV or fritter away too many mornings on the telephone?* Barbara doesn't know.

Why does she constantly feel as if she's running several days behind? Why does the ironing and housework and wash always pile up? *Maybe I should cancel my subscriptions to "Woman's Day" and "Family Circle,"* she thinks. *Maybe those magazines eat up too much of my time.*

But the problem is deeper than that. Barbara must learn to manage her time. She has a problem of focus; she is interested in so many things, but she finds it impossible to zero in on a single activity and make long-range accomplishments. Though each day is full, Barbara is running in place rather than moving steadily forward.

Bill Jarvis—A Successful Leader with a Need
for Priority Balance

Bill appears to be a striking success. His small sporting goods store, begun just ten years ago, has grown rapidly— even explosively. He now owns a chain of nine stores and has over seventy people on his payroll whom he must manage skillfully. He must be always mindful of new trends in order to direct his enterprise.

Not only is he skilled in business, but Bill is also creative. He enjoys a wide range of books, leads a study group in his church, and some day wants to write a book. And he will. He's the sort of person who can do what he sets his mind to.

Yet Bill knows the pressures and time demands he now faces will continue to lay heavier claims on him. He has risen, overnight it seems, to new heights of responsibility. He is now an executive facing constant decisions and unending demands for his emotional energy. He must now reckon with a budget of several million dollars, knowing that a tiny miscalculation can cost thousands at year's end. When his business was young, he could afford to take it a bit easier. Now, if he lets up he is quickly several days behind.

Bill is naturally a producer and an efficient organizer. Yet these natural tendencies are not sufficient to get done all that he faces in a day. Bill recognizes his need for greater productivity and wiser time use. He knows he needs to make better use of the people he has working for him. He was swept into his present position because of his interest in athletics and sports gear, but now he is doing far more each day than fitting jogging shoes. He manages people who must hire employees, and set expense percentage goals. There is much he needs to learn about working with people.

Bill is also concerned about his family. He does not want to put his wife and children in the back seat while he pursues prosperity and success. He needs to meet his growing business responsibilities and challenges while keeping his family at the center of his life. He knows fourteen-hour workdays aren't the answer. He needs something else.

Not only does Bill need to learn more about managing people, he needs to learn how to balance his priorities. He needs to know how to fit a very demanding life into each twenty-four-hour day.

Do any of these people sound familiar? Do the needs in their lives resemble your own? These dilemmas are universal. You, like each of these individuals, face the issue of TIME. You have only so much. How are you going to spend it? How are you going to cram all those things you want to do into each twenty-four-hour day?

Here is good news: there is enough time to accomplish everything you must, want, and even dream of. It isn't a matter of speeding up your metabolism so that you can work at a frenzied pace. You're going to discover that you can be *less busy* and have *more time* for enjoyable extras— yet *accomplish more than you do now.* Often the most productive people are those who appear most peaceful.

Two questions about time use and productivity must be asked. The first is, WHAT IS TO BE DONE? The second, WHAT IS THE MOST EFFICIENT WAY TO DO IT? Memorizing a bunch of time-use gimmicks won't necessarily lead to productivity. You must first have in mind what you want to accomplish (goals). You must then decide how to accomplish it (planning).

One person may have grand visions but lack the practical skills to bring them to reality. Another may be a highly efficient worker, but lack the foresight to set worthwhile goals. Neither will usually achieve all they would like to. It is instead, the man or woman who can blend both vision and efficiency into his daily routine who will know unusual success and accomplishment. It is the person who has goals *and* who can manage himself, his time, and other people who is destined for great productivity and significance.

One of the true tests of distinction in one's particular role in life is not status or magnetic personality; it is, instead, the capacity to accomplish a task. It has been said that there are but three types of people in the world: those who don't know what's happening, those who watch what's happening, and those who make things happen. Productive, accomplishing men and women are of the third type—*they make things happen.* It matters not whether an important title appears on an office door after one's name. Results, not labels, are the true measure of importance.

Anyone can learn basic skills which will enable him to accomplish more in his or her life. You may not be a natural leader with dynamic personality and impressive gifts, but if you want to accomplish something, you can begin to reach that goal.

This is the foundation on which this book is built—that accomplishment is within everyone's reach. It may be a large or a small thing you want to achieve. You may want to be a U.S. Senator or you may just want an opportunity to tell a neighbor about Jesus. It may or may not be connected with your vocation. A housewife will have family-related goals. Students and teachers will have school-oriented goals. Executives will have business-centered goals. Many of you will have things you want to accomplish in your churches and various relationships.

Deciding what you want to do and then using your time wisely to get it done . . . that's what we're going to discover how to do together. Want to accomplish more? You can!

Evaluate Yourself

1. Can I identify with the plights of the following people? What similarities exist between my situation and theirs?
   a. Pat Coleman (conscientious but frustrated, tired, isolated, unfulfilled).
   b. Dave Jenkins (stagnating on a plateau, lacking motivation, full of unrealized dreams).
   c. The Higdons (too busy and involved, lacking goals).
   d. Barbara Redmond (undisciplined, content, going nowhere).
   e. Bill Jarvis (in need of efficiency and priority balance).
2. Efficiency and productivity boil down to *having a job to do and getting it done.* What *exactly* am I trying to accomplish?

3. True distinction is not status or personality but the capacity to get something done. *Results* measure importance! Can I visualize myself as a person who can blend vision and practical skills to see goals reached? (This is the key to productivity and significance on the highest level.)

The capability to guide and direct a course of action lies open to all!

3. THE KEY—DISCIPLINE, EFFICIENCY, AND DECISIVENESS

We now plunge into the nitty-gritty of learning to do more, in less time, more efficiently. You now begin the task of retraining yourself in three fundamental areas—discipline, efficiency, and decisiveness.

Learn to Discipline Yourself

Self-discipline is the very tap root of success! It is the first step toward productive accomplishment. It must become evident in every area of your life—your relationships with God, your spouse, children, friends, associates; your personal study; your thoughts and habits; your goals and aspirations; your routines of diet, exercise, and sleep.

"Disciplined" means controlled, subject to order, not random or haphazard. There must be purpose and order in everything you set your hand to. Many people settle for mediocrity because they are unwilling to pay the price of such a disciplined life.

You may be complaining, "That's fine if you happen to be a naturally self-disciplined person, but I'm not. Discipline comes hard for me."

But a controlled life-style is not natural for anyone. Self-discipline is *never* easy.

Look at the definition again—"controlled." That implies there must be something to subdue. By its very nature discipline involves going against our natural tendency to be undisciplined and thereby controlling and subduing it.

31

We're *all* undisciplined by nature. The key to accomplishment is mastering that undisciplined nature, so we can put it to use and thus get done what we have to do.

Simply stated, *discipline is making yourself do something that doesn't come naturally*; it is making yourself do the thing which would be easier not to do. It's plain hard work!

Things just don't get done any other way. If you hope to float along into increased productivity, forget it. It'll never happen. When I surrender to the "float" mentality, I soon find myself in front of the TV, watching some program I don't even like. "Floating" leads in one direction—toward inefficiency. If you want to get *more* done, you must expend elbow grease, sweat, determination—elements of self-discipline.

Self-discipline comes down to that tiny, insignificant moment of decision. In that tiny moment you decide to either stick with your original resolve or take the natural, easy way out. We each face a thousand such moments weekly. Tremendous accomplishment or a commonplace life is determined right then.

If two men set as a goal to rise at 5:45 a.m. to study, pray, and seek God's direction for the day, neither will find it easy. Their natural tendencies will always be to sleep in "just this once." But the man marked for leadership, the man determined to reach his goal, the man destined for significant achievement, will *force himself* to get up and carry out his decision. It's no easier for him than for the other, but he has learned to overcome the inherent obstacles.

If two women each read a book on natural foods and think, "As part of my stewardship, I should be more conscientious about the foods I fix for my family," it will not necessarily be easy for either to lay aside old patterns in order to make beneficial improvements. But the woman who is disciplined will weather the difficulties of learning to cook and eat more nutritious food. She will not give up. She will *make herself* do what she set out to do.

After several years, self-discipline may look as if it's easier for the successful person. But that is only because he has trained himself for years (in rising earlier, in cooking healthfully, etc.) until the habits have solidified. Men and women who have made lasting accomplishments—inventors, missionaries, statesmen, evangelists, writers, athletes, and businessmen—have all learned (through discipline) to achieve nearly twice as much per day as the average person. The person set apart, like the skilled athlete, is constantly in training. He becomes master over his circumstances, which no longer dominate him.

Such self-discipline builds long-range perspective. The productive person develops staying power, persistence. He paces himself wisely and thus does not burn out prematurely. Howard Hendricks calls this, "bulldog tenacity . . . guts." He states, "The key to leadership is endurance," and admonishes, "Develop an unwillingness to throw in the towel."

The Lord needs men and women whose eyes are riveted on a goal and who resolutely move toward it. Christian activity, as in the impetuous lives of Pete and Cindy, can frequently be an up-and-down affair. Someone gets swept up in a new idea and it catches on. It takes the church by storm and everyone gets into the new program. But after a while the excitement wanes and there soon comes a new bandwagon to jump on. One can easily be distracted from ultimate goals by temporary ones. Yet such pell-mell motion is often a sign of undisciplined immaturity.

The Lord needs stable, mature, and disciplined men and women who are running toward the objectives He has given for them to reach. The Christian life is a marathon, not a 100-yard dash. I've run marathons and I can tell you, after fifteen miles there's no glory in it—it's just one foot in front of the other, mile after mile. (During every race I wonder, *Why do I run marathons?*)

But that's the way it is with any significant, long-range goal, whether it's related to business or to raising children. Everyone starts out in the same place under basically the same conditions, just as in a marathon. Some over-zealous, inexperienced runners cover the first several miles at six minutes per mile, not realizing how difficult it soon becomes to maintain such a blistering pace. But others—who know their own endurance, who understand the rigors of the course, who discipline themselves to maintain a proper pace—finish the race.

Opposition *always* sets in, whether you're running a 26-mile race, remodeling your kitchen, or building maturity and wisdom into your teenager. The same temptations to quit bombard everyone. To my knowledge, *everyone* in a marathon considers quitting. Some do quit, the finishers don't.

The significant, accomplishing person, be he marathoner or parent, refuses to buckle under the pressure. He doesn't quit. No matter how uninspired the moment, how commonplace the assignment, how tedious the chore, he endures to the end. That's self-discipline—*making yourself* do it, going on, enduring to the end.

A person's response to unrewarded and unrecognized drudgery reveals his mettle and fortitude, his capacity to view the goal through the dust of the daily grind. The productive person plods on toward his objective. He knows that reaching the finish will be his true reward.

Put Your Time to Its Most Efficient Use

Nowhere is discipline more evident than in controlled use of time. Time is our great, irretrievable commodity. Wasting it is the flaw of the individual who fails to reach the heights God has for him. This does *not* mean one should mortgage his family, friends, and personal growth in order to spend eighteen hours a day laboring at the office or that he should involve himself in church activities nightly. It means that the use of one's time is well planned and purposeful, not accidental.

Good time-use habits come only one way—through practice and hard work. No one has more time than anyone else. You cannot add to your daily twenty-four hours. This is all God has provided for you in which to do all He would have you do. Therefore you must learn to utilize it efficiently.

The distinction between a successful and mediocre existence is in those surplus minutes and hours which are either frittered away or afforded miserly care. The average working man spends seven to nine hours at his job and daily accomplishes, perhaps, five or six hours worth of meaningful work. The efficient person, however, at the job, at home, at school, or at the church, can extend his output to the equivalent of nine or ten hours during the same period. Apply this same criteria to your evening hours. How are they spent? "Extra" hours always exist. It's up to you to find and make use of them.

The more productive you determine to be the less you will measure your day by the time-clock. The time-clock mentality is concerned with total hours, coffee breaks, vacations, pay, and quitting time. Rather than seeking and creating ways to fill every moment to the full, people with this view point concern themselves with "being" there, getting through the day, logging so many hours on the time card. Many women spend their days at home in this manner as well, just putting in their time, waiting till the day is over rather than filling the day with productivity.

But if you desire to use your time efficiently, a certain span of time will be meaningless to you. You will measure time by what is *accomplished*. You will *fill* time, not just *endure* it. Thus you will eat lunch *and* read, drive *and* listen to a tape, wash the dishes *and* plan an afternoon activity with the children, drive to an appointment *and* plan what project to tackle when it is over. Every minute must count.

As you acquire this mentality, you will less often have to say, "I don't have time." It is never the most productive men and women who have no time; therefore, the leader in need will usually turn to the busiest individuals for help. Every church has people who are continually swamped, yet they are the first to be asked for assistance when a new need arises. When such individuals agree to accept a responsibility, it is usually carried out well. This is because their time is well ordered. They know what they can and cannot handle.

Certainly when you are busy and are intent on your duties, you will often have to say no. The ability to turn down countless offers is a mark of maturity. But you will rarely say no because you have no time, but rather because the activity itself does not contribute to the fulfillment of the particular objectives God has assigned to you. If the offer had been one that could have fit into your priority structure, you would have found the time for it.

We all use the same amount of time. Does your use of time propel you toward your goals or sidetrack you from them?

There are several key principles which can increase your efficiency. Commit the following list to memory and remind yourself often of these things:

To use time productively you must:

1. *Maintain a rigorous personal schedule with a regular routine.*
2. *Discover timesavers—use every little moment for something.*
3. *Put your time to double use.*
4. *Stay organized.*

Maintain a Rigorous Personal Schedule with a Regular Routine

Establish a regular daily schedule and stick to it

ruthlessly. This will insure that things will get done. Without a structure around which to plan and order your day, many seconds, minutes, and hours will be lost. The reason is simple. A regular routine decides in advance for you what you will do and when. You don't have to think about it and constantly weigh various options which are tugging for your attention. You simply *do* what your schedule tells you to do.

It may not seem that deciding when to get up and when to eat lunch would take that much time. But if these decisions take *any* time, that is time wasted. And not only do such little decisions take time, they each drain a bit of mental energy. Over the course of a day or week, such little robberies of your seconds and energy add up.

Determine to get up at the same time every day. Play handball or tennis or go jogging on the same three afternoons each week. Set a time for Bible reading. Plan to spend time talking with your husband or wife. Shop for groceries, do the laundry, and mow the lawn on the same days every week. If you establish such a schedule, there will be time for everything you want to do, because you have carefully constructed your schedule to incorporate all your priority items.

A schedule liberates you from guilt and frustration. For instance, if you have predetermined that on Thursday morning you will take the kids to the zoo and park, then no matter what the house looks like and no matter how high the dishes are stacked, you can guiltlessly pile into the car for a carefree jaunt. If Friday is your clean-the-house day, you don't even have to think about cleaning the house on other days, because your schedule has already allowed for it.

Regularity forces better time use. "I open and deal with my mail at 10:30, return calls from 1 to 2, plan the following day at 4, and jog at 4:30."

Or, "I wash clothes on Monday, go to a Bible study Tuesday morning and clean the bathroom in the afternoon, buy groceries on Wednesday morning and sew in the afternoon, take the children swimming on Thursday, clean the house on Friday, bake and do home-activities with the children on Saturday." With such decisions already made, your energy can be focused on *doing* them.

When our children were very young, Judy daily experienced frustration because she was unable to keep up with the household chores. She finally devised a weekly home-maintenance schedule and was thus liberated from the daily pressure of messes here, dirty clothes there, dusting to do over there. Knowing she would wash diapers on Monday and Thursday, clean the bathroom on Tuesday, buy groceries on Wednesday, vacuum on Friday, and bake on Saturday freed her from constantly wondering whether things would get done. The weekly schedule allowed her to relax, even if she missed something on its day, knowing it would be taken care of the next time around. After all, with a house full of children, if you miss the vacuuming today, will another week really matter?

There are many things you want to accomplish—rising a half hour earlier to read and study, spending an additional evening per week with your family, spending one afternoon every two weeks with each of your children, exercising two hours a week with a co-worker, plus many other important things. A pre-set schedule will not only help you complete your must-do jobs that are a normal part of each day, but also those things you want to add. *Your schedule can include anything you want.*

Setting up a schedule that helps you accomplish what you want to do—the must-do's as well as the extras—simply involves writing down all your potential activities and then working them into your particular time frame. Experimentation will be necessary. What you put down on paper will not always work out in practice. It may take some time before you arrive at a routine that works completely. You will not be able to attain everything at once. But the schedule is the starting point. It steers you in the proper direction—toward your goals.

Once your schedule is established, you must become tough and uncompromising. If you intend to follow the stringent guidelines you have set (except for higher priority items that arise unexpectedly), you must obey your schedule exactly. If you excuse yourself with, "Just ten more minutes in bed," or "Next time, Son; something's come up," or "Just one more TV program," or "Just fifteen minutes longer for lunch—I'll finish the report tomorrow," or "There's not that much laundry today so I'll squeeze it in tomorrow before I go shopping," you'll fall short of your goals.

Discover Timesavers

Time is a phenomenal thing. Staggering amounts can be accomplished with little pieces of it—if you use them regularly. For instance, one doesn't normally sit down and read through the Bible in one sitting. But with a minimal investment of ten to twenty minutes a day, you can read it through every year.

Doing anything regularly and steadily will achieve never-dreamed-of results. Think of all the empty moments you face—waiting for someone to come to the phone, sitting at a red traffic light, waiting in line at the bank, sitting in a dentist's waiting room, watching ads on TV. An enormous number of hours, over a lifetime, are seemingly void of any use at all. Just imagine what you could accomplish if you put those seconds and minutes to use.

You can discover the techniques for using those spare snatches of time regularly. Over the years they will result in extra days, weeks, even months of productivity.

The following are timesaving habits I've cultivated to use those little moments of otherwise zero-accomplishment. You will discover your own techniques as well. Consider such secrets prize gems, for they will eliminate your need to say, "Where did this day go?"

1. *Deal with things as soon as they come up.* Procrastination unnecessarily defrauds you of time. Make DIN (Do It Now!) your principle of action. Suppose your four-year-old comes to you and asks, "Mommy, can Jenny come and play with me?" Don't say, "Well, not today, but sometime soon." Instead, say, "Let's call her mother right now and arrange a time with her."

If your assistant comes to you and reports, "Mr. Barnes was in about his order. It's long overdue and he's pretty upset," don't reply, "Oh, uh, well, we'll have to look into it if it isn't in pretty soon. It'll probably be here in a couple of days." Instead, dig into the situation, call your supplier, call Barnes, and see the matter through to a conclusion. Only then will you keep customer problems from piling up.

2. *Focus on objectives.* When potential activities confront you, clear goals will help you know quickly whether they are things you should spend time on or dismiss. Learn to recognize those things you should *not* spend time on. Don't jump into something you will later drop as useless.

3. *Write things down.* Always have a list so you're never lacking something to do. Never be without pencil and paper. Use daily lists and calendars so you know what's coming—meetings, trips, activities, deadlines, projects, shopping lists.

4. *Fill odd moments.* Keep a book, New Testament, note pad, or simple project with you in case you must wait for five or ten minutes at the bank's window or at the doctor's office. If you can't actually *do* something, pray for the other patients, the doctor you will see, the person you are waiting for on the phone, or the construction workers who are delaying traffic. Any bit of time can be redeemed.

5. *Plan before jumping in.* The time and effort necessary for a job can be used much more effectively, and waste can be eliminated, when the necessary steps are planned. Ten minutes of planning can save thirty in execution. You can plan every activity (even those involving children),

phone call, appointment, and interview.

6. *Plan and use your evenings.* Evenings are wasted time for most people. If you have a family, evenings should generally be reserved for family-oriented goals.

7. *Analyze your time-use habits.* Don't allow days to simply slip by. Investigate wasted time and deal with it. Refine and improve your schedule. After all, having a routine doesn't mean living in a rut for the rest of your life.

8. *Focus on priorities.* Spend time on the highest priority item first (unless there's a good reason for delaying it). Don't bypass an important task to devote a large chunk of time to something far less important. Always ask yourself, "If I am interrupted from this job, what aspects of it do I want to make sure are done?"

9. *Don't get sidetracked by obstacles.* When stumbling blocks arise, deal with them. Don't allow them to drain your vitality.

10. *Force yourself to make decisions.* Delay eats up time. Stay well practiced in the (difficult) art of saying NO.

11. *Never forget Parkinson's Law—work expands to fill whatever time is available for it* (whether that much time is necessary or not). When you have a job, get it done! Don't let it take longer than it needs to. Skillfully set yourself deadlines.

12. *Keep your body in tune.* It takes vigor to maintain your routine. Get as much sleep as you need, but no more—early to bed and early to rise is still wise counsel. Don't get fatigued from either too little or too much sleep. If your work load is heavy, learn to catnap. Exercise is also an important element in sustaining an active pace, as is moderate eating (a full stomach can slow you down, so either skip lunch or eat a light one).

13. *Consider your frame of mind when selecting jobs.* Perform tasks at your optimum time for them. Tackle the most mentally taxing ones early in the day and reserve busy-work for later.

14. *Plan your errands.* Errands consume much time, but they are a necessary evil. Let them accumulate and then do several at once, thus keeping running around to a minimum. Keep your car tuned and drive during slack traffic times.

15. *Make seconds count.* Handle each piece of paper only once—deal with it the first time. Paper shufflers are rarely productive decision-makers.

16. *Move from interruptions right back to your work.* Don't let them derail your train of thought.

Put Time to Double Use

You cannot add to the number of hours available, but you can "stretch" twenty-four hours by performing more than one task in one block of time. Pack each moment to its fullest.

Just as a prism splits apart a beam of light into several parts, with some thought you can split apart a single piece of time into several parts, each of which you can use differently. The secret is in using the same segment of time to accomplish results in different areas. For example, we doubled the use of the time Judy spent on the telephone. We moved our phone into the kitchen and installed a long cord so she could work on a recipe, stir a batch of dough, or clean off the counter while engaged with a caller.

There are numerous possibilities here—memorizing scripture or planning a meeting while driving, shaving or washing the dishes; listening to music or special messages on cassettes while working in the garage; planning your next day during the dead time of a large meeting. I often work on some hand activity (we call them our "therapy crafts") while watching TV. The other night Judy and I watched a football game while canning ten quarts of applesauce. Judy is never without some needlework project she can work quietly on during a small-group discussion.

Driving is often a one-dimensional activity which accomplishes very little, but it can be a great opportunity for communication with your children. Just last night I took two of my boys with me on an errand which involved a half hour of driving. We had a wonderful talk about the moon, astronauts, and the Lord—a talk that we'd never have had if I'd gone alone.

I never go on a business trip without a batch of teaching tapes to play on the car-cassette or without specifying the time for some structured thought. Sometimes there are issues which need detailed thought which I haven't had time for. A long drive can be just what I need to gain some solid perspective.

Prayer and communication with the Lord can be done most anytime, once you begin to use the split-apart-a-piece-of-time-into-its-various-components principle. Invalids have huge blocks of time which often go totally unused, but prayer can transform such empty time into the most meaningful form of time-use of all. We have a 92-year-old friend who is confined to a nursing home. Her active days are over, but not her prayer life. Every time I see her she asks about many of my daily situations—in detail. She and I are close friends and she has taken it upon herself to pray daily for me and all the things I face. What a commitment!

An activity that has greatly challenged me to discover ways to use time more effectively has been my long morning runs. Some of my most fruitful thinking occurs during those hours. I also pray for my family as I run. But my greatest discovery has been a hand-sized, battery-operated cassette player which I strap tightly to the small of my back. I run a headphone cord up through my shirt. Now as I run I listen to tapes on personal growth, family life, or business. Sometimes I run to the music of Mozart, Strauss, Chuck Girard, or the Communion Album. If I pray during such times, or am stimulated into new areas of thought, I accomplish *three* things in one span of time!

These are some of *my* methods. You will discover your own. Use your ingenuity as a prism, splitting time apart to put it to double, or even triple, use.

Stay Organized

Some activists and visionaries think a great idea and continuous activity will get the job done. This is not so. Vision and enthusiasm become tangible results only through organized effort. Disorganization breeds inefficiency and wasted time.

This may seem a minor point, having to do with personality—but not so, even though organization comes more naturally to some than others. If you would put your time to productive use, you must cultivate the ability to administer the details of your life and surroundings. This involves more than having a desk, an in/out box and a file cabinet. It involves training your mind to be analytical and systematic and able to keep details straight. You must learn to think logically and communicate clearly. Mental organization, as any skill, takes practice.

Begin with the physical appearance of those areas where you spend most of your time. Every kind of work has its place, its "control center." For businessmen, pastors, professors, students and professionals, it's a desk. For housewives it is probably the kitchen and to a lesser degree a sewing table, laundry room or kitchen table. For others it may be a workbench or tool cabinet. Wherever you spend a great deal of time is for you the place to start.

In order to regularly accomplish work and to achieve visible results, you must create favorable conditions which make such work possible. That means a well-organized and tidy work area. An orderly and businesslike desk, counter or table will not only give you a place to work efficiently, it will inspire you to action. If you're proud of it, you will enjoy spending time there, doing what you like to do.

We've all seen desks that are piled high with mail, magazines, papers, boxes and trash; a little one-foot space is left on which the owner struggles (from lack of space) to get something done. Sloppiness just won't work. What man feels enthusiastic about getting a jump on the day when he is greeted every morning by two weeks' worth of unopened mail and unfinished paperwork? What woman feels elated about facing the new day when her kitchen contains so many unwashed dishes that she can't even find a place to set down a glass—without shoving back a plate, which then knocks a spoon onto the floor?

If you're going to produce, maintain a clean, shipshape area that is a joy to look at and use. I love to come to my desk each morning. Throughout the day, I pile it high and scatter things about, knowing that I am using it to the fullest and knowing that everything is exactly where I want it. When the day is over I put things tidily in order. I leave with a good feeling, knowing that a good day is behind me and another good day awaits me tomorrow.

Examine your attic, your closets, your garage, your laundry room, your miscellaneous drawers and cupboards, your tool shed. They will reveal your organizational needs very quickly. If you tend to accumulate junk you probably have some work to do. If something's not going to be used for five years, get rid of it. You'll be better off buying another if you should need one than to save it indefinitely—"just in case."

Concentrate especially hard on your particular work area—desk, file, bookcase, briefcase, countertop, garage. This is where "stuff" will automatically converge. If your desk has a vacant spot on it, the next armload will land there. Therefore, a one-time spring cleaning will not suffice. Additional daily things will try to worm their way in, adding to the clutter and slowing you down. Stay on top of the infinite details and *things* that crowd in upon your life, your schedule and your work area.

Determine not to be a pack rat. Strip your desk of all the junk you never use—rubber bands, three-inch pencils without erasers, 3 x 5 cards, stamp pads, cancelled checks, gas station receipts, old church bulletins, magnifying glass, paper clips, the keys to the footlocker and toolshed, and stapler (out of staples!). Whatever of these you want to save, put elsewhere, so you don't have to constantly rummage past it just to find a decent pen to use.

Both my wife and I follow these principles of organization, she at home and I at the store. The specifics differ, but the ideas remain the same. I have a monthly and daily list on top of my desk at all times. Judy operates from a daily and weekly planner on her kitchen counter on which she organizes everything she has to do—the week's dinner menus, the shopping list, activities and obligations, things that she is going to be doing with the boys. She even includes many of my activities on her list so she is prepared for them, even if it's just reminding herself that I'll be gone on such-and-such a night.

We recently remodeled our kitchen. The former layout made it impossible for Judy to work efficiently—the cupboards were poorly arranged, the space was badly organized, and there was little room for a table or eating area.

Since the kitchen is her work area and hub of activity, we planned the new design (same size, just different utilization) from the standpoint of work efficiency. We included a planning/desk area where Judy is able to do her paperwork and keep cookbooks. There is a baking center for bread-making which doesn't interfere with the rest of the counter space. Cupboard space fits into the work flow. The built-in table is arranged for effective before and after meal use with respect to the counter and sink. The stove, refrigerator, and bake area are coordinated. Foot traffic through the kitchen is no longer congestive. Every facet was carefully planned. Far fewer steps are now wasted and Judy is able to be more productive, simply because of an organizational change.

Detail consciousness and work-efficiency go hand-in-hand. Be constantly aware of the importance of details, for out of the abundance of a day's details comes efficient accomplishment—or large amounts of wasted time.

Be a Determined Decision-Maker

Prioritized time-use necessitates making decisions, judging quickly the relative importance of various possibilities. Decisiveness is a primary mark of the man or woman who gets things done. The knack for making decisions is not inborn but is, like discipline, acquired through practice.

Decisions never get easier "tomorrow." Although when facing them, it always looks as though such will be the case. It takes courage to make hard-nosed decisions between thorny options, to be decisive in the face of opposition. It takes courage to stand firm under pressure. It takes courage not to buckle under stress and adversity. It takes courage to chart an unfamiliar course. But in all situations, whether of everyday or crisis proportions, indecision leads to aimless wandering.

This does not mean you egotistically assume that every decision you make is a wise one, but that you simply have confidence in yourself and in what you are trying to accomplish. You must acknowledge that sometimes making a wrong decision and then moving on in the Lord's grace is better than to have made no decision and allow the work to grind to a standstill.

While the average man or woman shies away from stressful situations and knotty decisions, the determined individual seeks them out. He tackles them head-on.

A coach I once had instructed us, "When you're in a race and you come to a hill, pick up your pace. All the other runners will be slowing down to take it easy—that's the time for you to pour it on."

That's wise advice. Approach decisions like hills. When

they confront you, *pour it on!*

There will always be repercussions from the decisions you make. Pressure will exist both before and after. It is always easy to entertain doubts and think, *Did I make the wrong choice?*

But you must not allow such thoughts to push you back into indecisiveness. You must keep moving ahead. Except in unusual circumstances, once you have made a decision, don't vacillate and harbor second thoughts about what you have done. If you are living in daily obedience to God and have made the choice thoughtfully and prayerfully, then you can know that God will oversee your progress.

In the spiritual realm, *adversity signifies advance.* If there are no problems, no tensions, no uncertainties, things are not functioning according to the biblical norm. The more you try to accomplish things and the higher you set your goals, the greater the pressure you'll experience.

This constant battle builds a fighting spirit. Such a wholeheartedness will keep you from being thrown off target, especially when you must make decisions. You must learn to slough off tension, failure, and doubts. You must be confident enough to tackle the most difficult problems with a sense of challenge.

Sometimes a roadblock will require a period of reflection and re-evaluation; there you will stop long enough to weigh various alternatives before you proceed. Such periodic slowdowns can be a healthy investment of time. But when the assessment is complete, you must pick up the pieces, stand tall once again, and move out, confident that God's faithfulness and the job He has assigned to you are still intact.

The following are three key factors for effective decision-making:

Clarify Priorities

Among the most difficult of decisions are those regarding use of our time (What will I spend *this* hour on?)—if priorities and objectives are blurred. But the stress of such decisions is considerably reduced when priorities are in focus.

The most difficult decision regarding the use of time is not generally between a good thing and a bad thing. The hardest choice is between a good thing and a better thing, or between a better thing and the best thing. Howard Hendricks writes, "Every time I say YES to what I consider a better thing, I say NO to forty other things. Things that are good things, things I would like to do, would enjoy doing. But they do not fulfill my objectives and the leadership of the Lord in my life."

Clarity of priorities makes saying no far less agonizing. In order to spend the evening watching TV with my family or helping my son with a wood-shop project, I may say no to attending a meeting where a noted personality will be present. In such a case the higher priority is my family. Because this is clear to me, making the choice not to attend the meeting is quite simple. In a sense I have made the choice in advance, simply because of my priority structure.

There are other times when I must attend a meeting or be away from my family for several days. When this happens I confront a difficult decision—between two of the best, top-priority things God has placed within the sphere of my responsibility—my family and my business. Therefore, if I must be away, I compensate both before and after by spending great amounts of time with each of my boys.

You cannot do everything, so you must concentrate on those primary areas God has given you. Only so will you be able to ease the pressure of the innumerable attractive options that present themselves to you day in and day out.

Don't Expect to Vanquish All Doubts Before You Decide

You must be able to face a constant barrage of decisions

without battling heart-wrenching anxiety over each one. Impulsiveness is no sign of maturity, but for those frequent, daily decisions which you face by the hundreds, you must learn to make them quickly. Your time must be reserved for the more important matters. The occasional life-altering decisions with far-reaching consequences, however, possibly require months to seek the Lord's guidance. You must recognize that many decisions must be made without the benefit of 100 percent assurance that you are doing the right thing. Unless the decision is a major one, you just don't have the time to think through every pro and con for an hour.

This is very difficult for those who want to weigh every consequence of a decision as if it were a move in a chess game. But if you are in fellowship with God and are walking according to His principles, you usually possess the insight necessary to make good decisions. You can confidently make the choice that looks right according to your good sense. If you begin to get out of line, God will stop you or close the door.

Confront Decisions Head-On

Do not assume that the multitude of decisions you face are to be taken lightly. You simply must train yourself to make decisions as quickly as possible. Make *good* decisions; but make them *fast*. "When you come to a hill, pour it on!"

I have the daily opportunity to practice head-on confrontation with decisions when opening my mail. My business often receives twenty to thirty pieces a day, and it is challenging to sift the wheat from the chaff. The mail is important, yet not what I would term critically important. Therefore, it is good to practice on the bills, checks, invoices, junk mail, personal correspondence, catalogs, trade journals, and new product announcements. I look forward to that stack of mail every day. I cut through it as rapidly as I can, spending only a second or two in determining which things to file in the waste basket and which to study more closely after I have been through the stack once. I want to miss nothing of importance, yet I want to dispense with the job as quickly as possible.

This "exercise" keeps me practiced so that I am ready to face more weighty matters. Self-training in such small matters prepares me for those decisions of greater consequence which take more time.

Skill in making good, quick decisions is a result of experience and knowledge. Though sometimes quickly made, they are nevertheless well thought-out. An active mind anticipates many factors and can assess them on the basis of past experience. Therefore, what appears on the surface to be a decision made in an instant is in reality the final statement at the end of a long process of thought and evaluation. To make sound decisions, you must be mentally prepared for the choices demanded of you tomorrow. I am able to open my mail quickly because I have been practicing it daily for ten years.

There is more to productivity than discipline, efficiency, and decisiveness. Yet no person ever reaches even close to his potential if he does not acquire these foundational qualities. They are qualities you can begin to acquire immediately, no matter what your present circumstances.

Evaluate Yourself

Discipline
1. Am I training myself in the *small* areas of life? Is my life-style markedly different from the norm?
2. Do I set aside regular time to plan?
3. What are some of my disciplinary *strengths*? What are some of my disciplinary *weaknesses*?
4. Am I self-controlled? Resolute? Enduring?

Efficiency

5. Do I plan my days and weeks? Do I sense accomplishment daily?
6. Am I disciplining myself in the use of my time? How much do I waste? Am I "busy" getting nothing done?
7. Am I master of my time, or its slave? How do I spend my evenings?
8. I will begin to employ the following:
   a. Deal with things when they come up.
   b. Focus on goals, not problems.
   c. Stay well-practiced in saying NO.
   d. Write things down.
   e. Plan *everything*.
   f. Analyze my habit patterns.
   g. Keep priorities clear.
   h. Make decisions without delay.
   i. Memorize Parkinson's Law.
   j. Not be derailed by interruptions.
   k. Put time to double use.
   l. Keep my work areas organized and neat.

Decisiveness

9. Do I avoid decisions or am I training myself in quick, yet efficient decision-making? Can I cut through surface factors to the heart of an issue?
10. Can I be decisive in spite of complex factors? Can I maintain calm in the midst of a crisis?
11. Am I willing to risk some poor decisions to keep things moving? Am I willing to face criticism?

**COMPLETE WORKSHEET #1 AT THE BACK
OF THE BOOK.**

4. SETTING GOALS—DECIDING WHERE YOU ARE GOING

If you're going nowhere, you're certain to get there. Jesus' life and ministry show that He knew where He was going. Often, long before His disciples had an inclination of what was happening, He was moving toward His goal.

God wants goal-oriented people—people who see worthwhile goals, who submit their efforts to Him, and then go out to reach the goals. God wants people today like Caleb, who said, "I want that mountain" (Josh. 14:12). The Lord said of him, "My servant Caleb showed a different spirit: he followed me with his whole heart" (Num. 14:24, NEB).

Goal-oriented men like R. G. LeTourneau can change entire industries. Women, like the prophetess Deborah, (though it hadn't been done in the same way before), can exercise spiritual leadership. People like Hudson Taylor and his wife can affect entire continents. God wants courageous, goal-setting men and women, moving under the guidance of His Spirit, who can change the very tides of history.

You Are What You Think

Everyone has goals, of one kind or another. Yet for most they are rarely achieved, and then only haphazardly. Seldom do we see sustained definite progress toward a specific goal. Success is not luck. It must be carefully planned for. And it begins with setting goals.

Merely *having* goals can be as fuzzy and undefined as

53

wishful-thinking and daydreaming. We must do something far more dynamic than taking five minutes before each day to scribble down a quick list of what you have to do. We're talking about *setting* goals, about making the goal-setting and planning process an important part of your everyday efforts.

Those who have goals and who plan for their fulfillment control their circumstances and accomplish things, both secular and spiritual. Successful, goal-conscious men and women recognize that they can do or become whatever they choose. There is a biblical truth at the root of all achievements. It explains why certain men rise from ghettos to make millions. It explains why some women are outstanding mothers and others are not. It explains success in every field, from athletics to politics to industry. This remarkable principle, forming the basis for accomplishment, is found in Proverbs 23:7: *"For as [a man] thinks within himself, so he is"* (NASB).

Not only *are* we what we think about, but we can *become* and *do* what we think about. If we set our mind and heart toward something and believe strongly in it, it *can* become a reality!

The mind exerts a power over the physical world. A picture paves the way for the later physical reality. When God gives you a goal, you don't have to sit back wondering if it will come about. You can go right to work.

In any endeavor, to accomplish anything, you must have a blueprint providing a clear-cut picture of what you are trying to do. Whether your goals have to do with your personal, professional, or home life, the process is the same. You can apply these principles universally to all areas at once.

Drawing a blueprint for success requires a mind reorientation because most of us have not programmed ourselves for success. We need to train ourselves to think big, to think positively about ourselves and about reaching the goals we set.

Planning involves having a purpose and goal and then working "backwards," forming a plan of attack enabling you to reach the goal. For instance, a teenager may desire to "be a good football player." That's a worthy purpose, but it will do him little good in a game. If he expects to achieve his desire, he'll have to throw catchable passes (that's specific). To throw a catchable pass he needs to aim a ball with accuracy and rifle a hard spiral (that's more specific yet). To gain that accuracy, he needs to hang a tire on a rope in his backyard and throw a football through the tire for an hour a day.

He has now progressed from his general purpose to a concrete, measurable goal, and has devised a workable plan in the process.

Think concretely, advancing from the abstract tomorrow to the specific *today*. Always ask, "What can I do *now* that will set me on course toward where I want to be tomorrow?"

There's a lot of verbal "fog" floating about in Christian circles because of fuzzy, ill-defined purposes and goals. We talk about giving God glory, taking the gospel into all the world, and living God-honoring lives. But as long as such statements remain undefined, they are useless.

If goals are clear, effective plans can be formulated. If goals are muddled, achieving them will prove difficult. Like a ship's rudder, goals set our direction for the future. Without clear objectives to aim at, we are like marksmen with no target.

We have more control over our futures than most of us believe. God is at work in our lives; we *can* set lofty goals. Goals provide a way for us to respond to God's working out His plan in our lives. We can know what He is doing if we pray, "Lord, show me your will for my life. Point me in the direction you want me to go." Out of such a prayer will arise the goals He expects us to diligently pursue. The man or woman of God need not fear thinking big or dreaming of accomplishing great things.

Setting Creative Goals

The secret of accomplishment lies in goals that are big enough. Let yourself go! Allow your imagination to run wild. Courageously dream great dreams. Think creatively into the distant future. What do you *really* want to do and become in the Lord? Do you believe He is able to achieve it?

Imagination is the cornerstone of achievement. Most of us do not experience great fruitfulness because we have not cultivated our ability to dream purposefully. We live merely coping with the endless specifics of life, rather than standing back to examine the pattern into which they fit. Setting goals channels our imaginations and dreams into definite and directed paths. Focusing the imagination in a pre-set direction insures that actions will follow.

Christians are often reluctant to dream. They misunderstand the paradox that while God is sovereign, He has yet given men freedom to develop gifts and talents and to use them creatively—God often expects us to take a large share of the initiative in getting things done. There is no desire God has placed into a human heart for which He has not also provided the means to accomplish it.

Concentration and Determination

Once your imagination has created a specific goal, you must lock onto that clear mental image. Single-minded concentration on your one significant goal requires blinders against the distractions all about you. You must avoid detours, plodding continuously toward the target. Thomas Edison was once asked how he achieved so much. His answer was, "It's quite simple really. We each have eighteen hours in every day in which we may do something. You spend that time with a number of unrelated things; I spend it doing *just one thing.*"

Concentration requires selection. Jesus concentrated

His efforts on only twelve men. A gardener severely prunes so the sap can be concentrated in only a few vigorous limbs. Which things will you pursue? Many potential activities will tempt you, but you must narrow the field. The skilled archer doesn't gaze at the fields or trees; he rivets his eyes on the bull's-eye.

Singleness of purpose was Paul's secret—"This *one thing* I do. . ." (Phil. 3:13, KJV). Trying to do five things instead of one neutralizes one's focus. For example, water from a nozzle can be spread over a large area in a powerless spray, or it can be focused into a powerful single stream.

If my immediate goal is to deepen my relationship with my son by reading him a book, I will not achieve that result if I try at the same time to watch the news on TV, or think about some problem at work. If reading the book will move me toward my goal, I must concentrate on that one activity and block out other distractions.

The subconscious mind, incredibly powerful and creative, can help you to achieve your goals. The subconscious, like a computer, must be programmed. This is done by providing it with a clear mental picture, which is accomplished by concentrating intently on it. With that picture clearly focused in your mind, the subconscious will go to work. It will devise ways, day and night, to make that picture a reality. It will work to reach your goal even when you are not thinking about it.

Some of your most productive thinking can take place when the conscious mind is relaxed, allowing the subconscious to work unhindered. I'm sure you have found yourself waking from a sound sleep with some specific detail on your mind which you possibly hadn't thought about. For example, not long ago I delivered a job to a printer which he would be working on for about a month. My part of the layout was behind me and I forgot about it entirely. About a week later, in the middle of the night, I suddenly awoke realizing I had left out one very tiny, but important, detail. I

58

had been completely unaware of my omission, yet the idea came so forcibly to my mind that it woke me from a sound sleep instantly. The following morning I hurried to the printer, just in time to make the change.

We'll never reach our goals by conscious thinking alone. We must allow the Holy Spirit to work through our subconscious minds to make great things happen.

Single-focus thinking is where it starts. Once you visualize a goal, concentrate on it and pursue it with persistent, dogged determination. The tale of the tortoise and the hare is relevant for today's productive man or woman. Achievement is 2 percent rabbit inspiration and 98 percent turtle perspiration.

Like the continual dripping inside a cave which forms huge mineral columns, the relentless pursuit of a goal produces results otherwise impossible. Goals direct your efforts, concentration locks you on target, and determination leads to success. Success waits for the determined, not for the gifted.

Negative thinking and discouragement are the universal hindrances to motivation. *Anticipate* fear, worry, and frustration. But do not let them deprive you of the energy you need to persistently stalk your goal. Deal with the problems maturely. But then move on without allowing them to affect your thinking permanently.

Martin Luther King's passionate, "I have a dream," has been echoed throughout history. Men and women from all walks of life have had "dreams" to perfect an invention, to attend college, to work on the mission field, to build a school, to explore an unknown frontier, to write a novel, to put a child through college—which were eventually realized because they determined never to give up until their dreams became realities.

Jimmy Carter's phenomenal drive from obscurity to the Presidency in 1976 and the Apostle Paul's worldwide impact for Christ in the first century are perfect examples of the results of determination. They visualized the end result in their minds. They believed confidently in what they dreamed, despite overwhelming obstacles, even despite all reason. They concentrated on their goals, devised strategies to reach them, and then followed those plans persistently. The results are history.

Will

What do you do when you awaken one day to find your desire cold, your vision faint, your motivation low?

Fortunately success is not founded in such emotions but in a much more stable characteristic, one not subject to daily fluctuating moods. This characteristic is your *will*— deciding that you *will* reach the goal.

Most people have not learned to discipline their wills. They follow desire instead. But desire is not will, for will can function when there is no desire. You command yourself into action through willpower as *you* choose, no matter what emotions are present or absent. When you command your will, you direct your course. Resolve and determination begin the process. Then the will takes over and plows through difficulties and hardships.

Many complain of weak wills, thinking this excuses their lack of discipline. *But there is no such thing as a weak will.* The will is strong by nature. But *discipline* can be weak. And when discipline is weak, the will remains untrained and therefore ineffective. The person moving toward accomplishment must control and dominate his will through self-discipline.

Dreaming is a good and necessary beginning for success. And praying is a vital part of it. But if there's something God wants you to do, you must translate that worthy objective into concrete action. This you do by applying your will. You must eventually say, "Okay, this is what God is calling me to do. The way is clear. I'll set some specific goals, plan it out, and then *do* it!"

This applies to anything—starting a Bible study, visiting the sick regularly, having a family prayer time, expanding your business, organizing a week of special meetings, starting an exercise program, initiating a family game night, returning to school for your master's degree, moving your church ahead into a neglected area of ministry though some of the leaders are content with the status quo, or spending 30 minutes a day reading to your children. If there's a goal to be reached, your will insures that it is reached. When obstacles rise and motivation drops, apply your willpower and KEEP GOING!

Nehemiah's Wall, an Accomplishment of the Will

Willpower, thoughtfully and diligently applied, day after day, leads to results. The question isn't whether you're going to lose your initial spark of motivation. That's certain to happen. The question is, what are you going to *do* when it happens—give up, or apply your willpower to get the job done anyway?

The reason for using our wills, of course, is that the Lord is directing our efforts. This was how Nehemiah approached the task God had given him. God gave him a vision of rebuilding the wall around Jerusalem. But Nehemiah didn't wait for God to do the job. He committed his way to the Lord, then set himself to do it. He planned out the job, drew diagrams, gave the people their orders, and made sure they followed through.

In a sense, it was a very "unspiritual" project. It was hot, sweaty work. Sore muscles, tired feet, bruised knuckles, smashed fingers, and daily frustrations were all part of it. But God had said, "Build the wall," and from that point on, it was simply a matter of determined obedience. Nehemiah did not have to go to the Lord every day or two for reaffirmation of that original vision, although when problems arose, he would go to Him for specific guidance. But beyond that, his only responsibility was to see that the objective was reached. Nehemiah exercised his will—and the wall was built.

You don't have to be a Christian to see the results of disciplined resolutions. But they only reach their greatest fulfillment when the decision-making process and the application of the will is in line with God's leading. God's part and ours go hand in hand. There is a tight and inseparable interplay between God's guidance and our actions. We make a decision and our will carries it out. Yet God must be behind our decisions, endowing our will with power.

Decision

The will is the boiler room of the mind where power is generated and where accomplishments are begun. Its enormous resources are harnessed and set in motion by a singular mental act *we* must carry out—the act of decision. Decision is the on-switch. It engages the entire dynamic process.

Decision of this kind is not "choice"—choosing between several options (What will I have for lunch today? What kind of car will I buy? Should I wear this pair of slacks or that pair? Shall I read or go to bed?). Decision is a firm, irrevocable determination to move in a certain direction. It is absolute and binding. There is no turning back. In the act of decision itself you resolve that you *will* stick to it. You decide that you *will* reach a certain goal, you *will* get there in the end, and nothing will stop you.

The failure to recognize the tremendous power God places in our hands through the decisions we make handicaps many Christians. Because God is sovereign, they hold that most of life's details are up to Him. When their plans are thwarted, it is God's will. When they get sick, it is God's will. When things don't go well in their families or their jobs, it is God's will. When their children turn out differently than they had hoped, it is God's will. When their marriages flounder, it is God's will.

Certainly God weaves His will through the details of daily life, and He can turn all things to good. But often implicit in such attitudes is the nebulous idea that we are to simply drift along, taking whatever comes without assuming personal responsibility for our own circumstances. Christians can be very reluctant to hold themselves accountable.

Many of us have therefore not been taught to realize that we can *decide* to accomplish some goal in our family or on the job, we can *decide* to improve a certain relationship, we can *decide* to make a shaky marriage work, we can *decide* to raise godly children, we can *decide* to reach people in our community for Christ, we can *decide* to reflect the character of Jesus. Within the boundaries of God's preeminence in our lives, we can *decide* to take control and responsibility over many of our daily circumstances.

The sum total of our individual decisions makes us what we are. God allows circumstances to mold, perfect and strengthen us. But our responses to those circumstances are the determining factor. We determine what sort of people we will be and what we will do by the decisions we make.

It's easy to overlook the critical role of personal decision which is illustrated in the Bible. For example, after Moses died, the Lord instructed Joshua to cross the Jordan and take the land. But it was the choices of Joshua and the Israelites that determined what land would be theirs. They, not God, were to decide:

> Now then, you and all these people, get ready to cross the Jordan River into the land I am about to give to them. . . . I will give you every place where *you* set your foot. —Josh. 1:2, 3 (NIV)

The Lord gave them the land by His power, but they decided which land to take. Their steps came first, His provision followed.

An often neglected word in the early chapters of the Scriptures is "dominion." God gave man authority over all things on the earth at the time of creation. God did not say, "I'll provide your food, name your animals, till your soil, bake your bread, and raise your children." No. God made it clear that man himself held influence in the world. He gave us, at the beginning, the capacity to make decisions which would forever alter the course of our lives and future lives— ". . . fill the earth, subdue it, take dominion over it, rule it" (Gen. 1:28).

God gave man *dominion*—over himself, over the earth, over circumstances. As Adam and Eve demonstrated, this great responsibility can be used against God just as readily as it can be submitted to His leading. The responsibility of how we use our dominion is ours.

Arriving at Specific, Useful Goals

Now that we've discussed the importance of setting goals, it's time to focus our attention on the actual process of formulating them. We need *specific* objectives.

Well-written goals must be:

1. Specific and understandable, with measurable end results.
2. Practical and achievable in a stated amount of time.
3. Written in precise language, using figures, dates and amounts—worded to avoid misunderstanding.
4. Limited (yet providing all necessary information) to a single objective; not long, complex, and ambiguous.
5. Firm, yet not frozen; reviewed periodically, yet not changed quickly or capriciously.
6. Clear statements about *exactly* what conditions will exist when the goal has been reached.

There may be a number of major areas for which you will establish goals. These might include: professional ambitions, family relationships and growth, personal spiritual growth, church and ministry, travel, personal reading, hobbies, exercise, finances, recreation. In all these areas of life, you already have some general purposes and aspirations. Therefore you need to construct some concrete goals which will see those purposes accomplished.

Suppose you set a goal to read fifty books this year. That is a good, specific, measurable objective which contributes to a greater purpose we all share—to be well-rounded, informed, growing Christians, with minds stimulated by fresh and new ideas.

So far so good. Long-range objective: read fifty books.

Now, how do you go about accomplishing it? You need some intermittent goals, consistent with the long-range objective, that will keep you on target. A good intermediate goal would be to read one book per week—a good standard that will keep you progressing regularly.

But you need an even shorter-range goal. So, after analyzing your reading speed and your schedule, you conclude that you must daily read approximately 45 minutes to an hour to finish a book each week. This is a goal for *today*.

You have now set three levels of goals:

Long-range—Read 50 books this year.

Intermediate—Read one book per week.

Immediate—Read 45 minutes to an hour per day.

You are well on your way, but at this point other factors will enter the picture—finding time to read, deciding what to read, where to read, how to read (study and note-taking, etc.), how to insure you don't quit, etc. A specific plan of attack is needed which will guarantee that your three goals will be reached. You will need to make some priority decisions about your time, you will need a plan, and you will need to exercise your willpower to carry out the plan day-after-day.

You can see that setting the goal is an important first step. For if you vaguely said to yourself, "I should try to read fifty books this year," and relied on whether or not you felt like reading every night before going to bed, the chances would be very slim that you'd come even close to reaching your goal.

With a clear objective and a plan to reach it, you can know with a certainty, *if you fulfill your daily goal, you will reach your yearly goal.*

Let's review the principles for setting and reaching goals:

1. Clarify your purpose, the general direction in which God is directing you to go.
2. Picture your situation in your imagination, not as it *is* but as it *can be.*
3. Engage your mental powers of concentration, determination, and will. *Decide* that you are going to reach the goal.
4. Establish long-range goals.
5. Set intermediate goals you must accomplish to reach the long-range goals.
6. Set immediate goals, things you must do now in order to reach the intermediate and long-range goals.

Evaluate Yourself

1. What do I want to *do* and *become*? I am what I think. I can do or become what I focus on.
2. When I daydream, what does my mind visualize? Have I ever considered pursuing some of those dreams?

COMPLETE WORKSHEET #2 AT THE BACK
OF THE BOOK.

5. PRIORITIES—LIFE'S GREAT BALANCING ACT

Once you've established goals, you need to consider what is the most expedient way to reach them. This involves selection. Which will you tackle first? How will you order your efforts in different areas? How do your various objectives fit together?

We all face time pressures. The person who would achieve success simply must determine how his time is to be spent. He cannot allow these pressures to dictate what he will do. He must control his time by setting meaningful priorities.

Many so-called "schedules" are directed by the constant call of urgent matters. People love to fight fires, dealing with one emergency, then racing off to face another. But urgency is rarely an indication of importance. In fact, the truly important matters (because they are long range in nature) are not usually as pressing as a stopped-up toilet is. If you are forever grappling with daily crises, you will never get to those important things needing your attention.

There are two aspects to priority selection. You must first decide which of your many potential goals you will pursue. Once you have narrowed the field, you then must balance those various things you have determined to be worthwhile.

What to Pursue—Which Potential Goals Will Become Your Priorities?

The creative person will usually have more in his head

that he would *like* to do than he realistically *can* do. There is no limit to the mind's capacity to envision worthy objectives. But there is a limit on an individual's time, energy, and resources. The wise person, therefore, does not automatically pursue every exciting new idea that pops into his head. He considers the larger picture; he weighs every potential venture against the overall scheme of the Lord's direction in his life. He lets his ideas season.

Out of life's many good and worthy goals, which do *you* concentrate on? Time is too valuable to squander. You must know that you are spending your time on the best and most important activities. When facing a new project, you must always ask, "Is this part of the larger purpose to which I am committed? Will it really matter if it isn't done? If it must be done, must I be the one to do it?"

This is the crux of Pete and Cindy's problem. Their lives are hectic but unproductive because they've been swept into every activity that presents itself. They haven't taken the time to determine which (out of the multitude of good enterprises) they *really* want to accomplish. Theirs is a problem of goals and priorities. Because they have no clear goals, they find it impossible to prioritize their many activities. Therefore, they do everything but get very little done.

Priority selection is knowing when to say no and saying it firmly and ruthlessly. You *have* to say no if you intend to focus your energies on the major, highest priority items which you are called to achieve.

Balancing Life's Diverse Goals

Once you have eliminated those things that do not contribute toward your ultimate purposes, you have to prioritize your time for those that remain. How do you fit together all those things you have said yes to?

The men and women God uses live balanced lives. They are motivated in many directions. They make lists of books they want to read. They maintain a Scripture reading program. They work to deepen their trust in God. They build certain qualities into their children's lives. They work to deepen communication with their spouse, always striving for quality time together. They strive to improve the quality of their work, and seek God's guidance for their vocational responsibilities.

Once you have decided which specific things to concentrate on, how do you fit them all together? They are all high priorities, so you must *balance* them. When you're facing a day's Things-to-Do list, it can be relatively simple to check items off one at a time. But weighing the important aspects of life is more complex.

Bill Jarvis, for example, is having to evaluate and balance his schedule and priorities. Unlike Pete and Cindy who haven't yet determined when to say no and when to say yes, Bill has basically already made those decisions. He is a successful leader precisely because he has already narrowed his focus to those key areas which affect his goals. Yet because of his demanding involvements, he is struggling with the second phase—balance. Knowing when to say no and when to say yes is only half the battle. From there he must equalize his life among all the yes's.

How do job, family, and church priorities balance so that all your goals are fulfilled?

I, for instance, operate four Christian bookstores, maintain a writing schedule, run five to ten miles a day, attend to my personal relationship with the Lord, fulfill church obligations, participate with my wife in a church family fellowship, teach at a lay school of ministry in our area, take viola lessons, try to cope with our boys' confusing array of allergy and learning disability problems, and spend time daily with my wife and three boys—next to God, they are my highest priority. Before I can even begin to launch toward my many objectives in each of these areas, I have to establish an equilibrium between all of them. I have important goals in *all* these areas—and others. Fitting them into each 24-hour day is difficult!

It's not as simple as, "If these two things were lined up alongside one another, which would be most important? Which would I concentrate on and which would I disregard?" I can't do that. I need to, if possible, reach all my goals.

If you have worked your way through the yes/no dilemma of sorting out many potential activities and now have some clear-cut objectives, "What will I neglect?" is no longer a useful question. This question should already have been dealt with. By the time you reach this point, all your goals should be important ones which you intend to reach. If you are where God wants you, then you mustn't neglect any goals, though your emphasis may shift at different times.

What is the key to balance? It is the realization that your time *must* be split up, apportioned relative to the objectives vying for your time. Clarify priorities and thus keep too much time from going one place at the expense of another. Some areas will take larger chunks than others, but you must determine how this allotment of your time will be parcelled out.

For example, I usually write in the morning and take care of store business during the middle part of the day. Therefore, after 4 o'clock each afternoon, my boys can have all of me they want without fear of intrusion. I have learned to put on and take off the various "hats" I wear.

Because I am operating at a high level of accomplishment, I can't afford the luxury of having only one thing to think about. When I have a job before me, I must give it everything I've got. I try to pack every hour with at least two hours worth of work. As I write this it is 5 a.m., and I have been up working for some time. In another hour I will go out for an 8-mile run and be back and showered by the time the family is awake. Once the house is astir I will shift gears. I will put on a different hat. No longer will my "productivity" be turned on. I will enjoy a relaxed breakfast and we'll talk and play for maybe an hour. Today I take one of my boys with me to the bookstore for a few hours, during which time I will accomplish little.

Whatever I have before me, I give it my all—whether it be running a race, reading to my boys, planning the budget for our stores' Christmas season, counseling a disturbed young man temporarily living in our home, working on a viola/harp duet with my wife, or preparing a detailed proposal to my church's board of elders. But the areas must remain balanced so they do not interfere with one another. I have to wisely maintain *all* aspects of those responsibilities the Lord has given me.

Priorities help me sort out the many demands on my limited time. I often need to juggle activities and to reschedule. There are times when selection between high and low priorities is a simple matter of relative importance. For instance, I have set myself a goal to read daily to my boys. Bible reading and general reading are part of each day too, but reading to my boys is the *most* important, the highest priority. In this case where the priority is easily visible, the decision is made for me in advance on the basis of what I have decided must come first. If I don't have time for all my reading, I read to my boys.

But there are times also when no alternative is obviously supreme. Is jogging, mowing the lawn, or taking my family out to dinner most important? The question is pointless because these matters are unrelated, there is no overlap. If I organize my time prudently, I should be able to do them all.

My life is full to the brim with activities and interests. My mind never stops dreaming up things to do. I therefore have to schedule those things I decide are important and fit them all into a day so that I work consistently toward all my goals.

Balancing goals and priorities creates a tension. The

involved person will always experience pull in many directions at once. Jesus experienced this tension, yet He didn't try to escape it. Suppose you had asked Him, "Which do you consider most important—ministering to people, teaching your disciples, or spending time alone with your Father?"

What do you think His answer would have been?

His answer would undoubtedly have taught us much about balance, for Jesus left both disciples and crowds to pray. Yet He willingly and eagerly ministered to them when they cut His prayer time short. He withdrew from the crowds with the twelve, yet He took every opportunity to heal and teach whenever the crowds followed.

In the life of Jesus we see perfectly exemplified balance of purpose. The tension was there. There probably were needs which were unmet, teaching for His disciples which went unsaid, prayers to His Father which were unfinished. He said no to many things. His purpose on earth required careful progress toward different goals, among men who did not recognize His purpose. Yet, though His time was so limited, at the end of His life He confidently declared that His purpose had been fulfilled.

Moderation and Balance

This book is primarily on productivity and efficiency—successful time-use. But unless you are obeying God in even the small areas of life, these principles of accomplishment can lead you astray. While the principles of goal-setting and planning can be put to work to make you a millionaire, such is not God's primary purpose in most cases.

This is a fatal error many "successful" men make. Men succumb to it more easily than women, although women are not immune. When they reach the end of a fruitful professional life, they suddenly realize that they have spent the bulk of their life chasing (successfully) the wrong goals.

Many, for instance, have no deep relationships with their children; and their money, prestige and position are powerless to change that situation.

It is not only money that deceives. How many women put all sorts of things above the time they spend with their youngsters? How many pastors have sacrificed their families for the sake of their ministries? If Satan can drive a wedge between what you want to accomplish and your family, he will.

Because we are discussing achievement and accomplishment, do not assume these to be the whole of God's pattern for success. There is much more to a fulfilled life than this particular area on which we are focusing. We should heed the following admonitions by James Dobson and Pat King as we balance the priorities in our lives.

For Fathers

Dr. James Dobson, one of America's foremost spokesmen for the family, makes this urgent plea to Christian men on one of his tapes:

> I went before the Lord and I asked Him to give me *his* message for the American family . . . and this is what He gave me . . . and it's primarily a message to husbands and fathers. . . .
> I really believe that if the American family is going to make it in the next ten years, it will be because husbands and fathers order their priorities in such a way that their families have a place and that their wives have a place and their children have a place.*

He later reads a portion of a letter written to him by his father at a time when, as he later realized, he was being swept into over-involvement with his career at the expense

---

* "God's Message to Christian Fathers"—cassette tape from the series *What Wives Wish Their Husbands Knew About Women* by Dr. James Dobson, Vision House Publishers, Santa Ana, CA.

of his children. This is what his father said:

> One of the great delusions is to assume that children
> will be devout Christians because their parents have been,
> or that any of them will enter into the Christian life in any
> other way than through their parents' deep prayer of tra-
> vail and faith. But this prayer demands time. Time that
> cannot be given if it is all signed and conscripted and laid
> on the altar of career ambitions. And failure at this point
> for you would make mere success in your occupation a very
> pale and washed out affair indeed.*

For Mothers

Pat King, who has written an excellent book for women
on time-use, gives this insight into the conflict of daily pressures vs. eternal values:

> How does a Christian mother find enough time . . . ?
> The basic fact is this: *children take time.*
> Therein lies the misery. There is so much we want to
> do, so much needing to be done in this world of ours, so
> much that society insists that we must do. We must not
> have ring-around-the-collar, we must have floors that
> gleam until we can see our faces in them, we must have
> furniture that reflects an arranged bouquet in living color.
> We must cook gourmet meals, be publicly aware, socially
> active, academically current. Then, of course, we have the
> children to take care of and the children take so much
> time.
> Training up a child takes time . . . discipline takes
> both time and energy, and instruction in the Lord must go
> on and on.
> As we add training, disciplining, and instructing to the
> list of feeding, cleaning, teaching, listening, and support-
> ing, it's easy to see why we may be miserable. All these
> things that must be done with our children are at war with
> all that society tells us, or that we tell ourselves, we must
> do elsewhere.

---

* "God's Message to Christian Fathers"—cassette tape from the series
What Wives Wish Their Husbands Knew About Women by Dr. James
Dobson, Vision House Publishers, Santa Ana, CA.

For me the war ended abruptly and with it, the misery, with the realization that I didn't have to be any of those people that magazines so subtly insisted I should be. I didn't have to be a great housekeeper or an enviable cook. I didn't have to wear any of those "hats" that the good people at our church thought everyone should wear, that of teacher, organizer, committee member. I didn't have to be any of the women that the school and the media insisted were so important: the politically involved, the champion of the downtrodden, or even the exciting, innovative hostess. . . .

If we have been called by God to be mothers, let's drop all the activities that are making it so painful for us to enjoy our children. ... *Let's give our children the time they need to help them grow into secure people.**

A Relaxed Balance

The Christian who would lead God's people by the example of his own life must apply the principles of success in his family life, as well as in other areas. Throwing ourselves into the attainment of certain goals does not imply we are to be at full-throttle, keeping an impossible schedule every waking moment. One of our goals must be the living of a rounded, temperate, balanced, peaceful life, centered around one's family. The Christian has a broad base of important things in his life; there is no single, supreme, consuming goal for which all else in life is thrown aside.

My home life is one of my prime concerns. Therefore, washing dishes, tending the garden, making repairs, shopping with Judy and the boys, changing diapers, helping with the laundry, and piling in the car to chase the fire engine are not sidelines which detract from my "calling." In the alignment of my priorities, these things are on an equal, if not higher, plane than my professional goals.

I realize that by the world's standards I could succeed in

How Do You Find the Time by Pat King, Aglow Publications, Lynnwood, WA. pp. 49-52.

far greater ways than I ever will. In fact, I cannot say I am unaffected by the lure of the world's standard of success. Because I am involved in business and financial matters, I cannot help but feel the lure of success and power gnawing at me. But, as a Christian concerned with the spiritual welfare and future of my children, the price tag for such success is too high.

Let's review what we've just discussed. *Setting goals* focuses us on what we want to accomplish. *Priorities* organize our many objectives and provide balance. Now we must jump headlong into the actual reaching of a goal.

The secret to getting from here to there lies in . . . THE PLAN!

Evaluate Yourself

1. What are the two steps in my priority selection process?
2. I now review my list of goals and objectives. Which things are high priority items? Which are low? If my available time were suddenly cut in half, which would I leave out?
3. How will I fit all my important goals into each 24-hour day? Are there conflicts anywhere in my schedule? Can I devise a workable framework that balances everything?
4. Can I realistically hope to achieve my goals in every area of my life? Does my life reflect moderation and balance?

I can't do everything. I must focus on my most important objectives. Therefore, out of life's many potentially worthy goals, what do I concentrate on?

6. PLANS—THE SECRET FOR REACHING YOUR GOALS

Your *goal* is the end result—what will exist "some day." But your *plan* tells you what to *do*—right now, tomorrow, next week, next month, until one day, lo and behold, you have reached your goal! The plan turns the goal into reality. It is a prescribed process which gets you from where you are to your target.

Some plans are complex, others are simple. The simplest of all may be a recipe—"Put ½ cup oats into . . . mix with . . . stir . . . add to . . . spoon onto . . . bake for 15 minutes at. . . ." These are very concise instructions. In about an hour's time you have moved from nothing (an empty cookie jar) to your goal (a full cookie jar). You had a goal. You followed a plan. You brought the goal into reality.

A plan is a staircase, each step leading to the next. You take one step at a time, following the instructions. No matter how high the flight of stairs and how lofty the goal, eventually you will reach the top.

The more detailed the plan, the more thorough will be the project's outcome. But writing plans is hard work! Thus, most people fail to plan at all and instead allow the random flow of circumstances to dictate the pace and direction of their lives. But though planning *takes* time, in the long run it *saves* time. A job that ordinarily might require an hour can usually be cut to thirty minutes, if ten or fifteen minutes are invested in carefully planning each step. Imagine trying to make oatmeal-raisin cookies without a recipe or trying to build a house without a blueprint. It just won't work.

Write the Steps Necessary to Reach the Goal

Planning involves nothing more than constructing a progressive list of what you must do. Each step builds upon the next. The more specific your goals, the more easily plans are formulated. Imagine a flight of stairs with three landings at intervals on the way to the top. These are intermediate goals en route to your final destination. If you have carefully set goals and have provided yourself some intermediate objectives, your planning is already half completed. All that remains is to fill in the gaps.

If I want to travel from Seattle to Miami, I have a very precise objective in mind—Miami. Without a roadmap, however, I am unlikely to reach it. In addition, I need intermediate goals along the way—Salt Lake City, St. Louis, and Atlanta. Once I am at this stage, I need to formulate a definite plan of action, which would include type of transportation (car, bus, bicycle, train), time of departure, stops along the way, timetables for each day's progress, arrangements for lodging (camping, motels, relatives), points of interest to visit, and a budget.

Any craftsman approaches a new project in the same manner. If the actual building of a desk, for example, was going to take 30 hours, the planning process could well take 3 to 5. Yet that investment at the beginning insures that his 30 hours will be used efficiently. It also guarantees that the completed desk will indeed look as he had originally drawn it. Without a detailed plan he could be certain of neither. His work could wind up taking 40 or 50 hours and the desk could turn out altogether differently than he had hoped.

After such careful planning, all that remains is to jump into action. One step at a time, we simply progress through our predetermined list, carrying out our plan by doing each thing in its proper order. When the final task on the list is completed, the desk is made, the cookies are done, the house is built, we have arrived in Miami—the goal is accomplished.

Before Nehemiah knew whether he would ever have the opportunity to go to Jerusalem, he had thoroughly investigated and planned his potential assignment. His thoughts were organized and he was ready in advance.

When the opportunity did come and the king asked Nehemiah what he wanted (Neh. 2:4), he was prepared. He did not stutter around the issue with vague spiritual generalities. He had studied the situation and his reply was well-formulated and specific: "I'll need letters to the governors beyond Euphrates for safe conduct; I'll need a letter to Asaph for the lumber necessary to make beams for the gates of the citadel adjoining the temple, for the city wall and for my home" (Neh. 2:7-9).

Nehemiah had done his homework and was confident. He knew how long the job would take and what would be needed. The king was so impressed by Nehemiah's readiness that he immediately sent him off to begin the project.

A step-by-step plan is an amazing thing! If well formulated, you can literally bring results out of nothing. Consider for example, John Kennedy's pronouncement in 1960—we will put a man on the moon in ten years. Lofty? Unattainable? Unrealistic? Certainly! It was clearly an impossibility.

But a plan was devised to bring it into the realm of the possible. Intermediate goals were established, preliminary space flights were taken; rockets, boosters, and fuels were improved and enlarged; sophisticated guidance systems were developed; procedures were outlined for each tiny aspect; and target dates were set. The specific vision of a man on the moon was kept in the forefront of everyone's thinking. There were incredible unknowns, setbacks, obstacles, questions. There were millions of details to consider.

But because every principle of successful planning was employed, at each stage, Neil Armstrong stepped onto the moon on July 20, 1969.

Building a Bookshelf

Setting goals and making plans is not only for important, far-reaching matters, but also for daily, even commonplace projects. For example, when I need a new shelf for our store, the first thing I do is visualize it. I turn it over and around in my mind's eye, trying to visualize it clearly—full of books. Then I sketch it. This is important, for the drawing will provide the basis for the entire project.

Once I am satisfied that the drawing is complete, I detail the steps I will take. I write down everything I will need. My drawing is specific and it tells me the dimensions of each section, so I calculate how many 1 x 12's and 1 x 6's I will need. I list the types and amounts of nails, sandpaper, stain, and varnish. I list every item I will need to buy. I ask myself about related items. What changes should I make in the shop for the job? Are the saw blades sharp? Are my tools in good condition? Will I need to borrow any tools? When will I do the work? Will I need some extra help at the store while I am building?

Then I list the steps needed to actually construct the shelf—which cuts to make (and in which order), which edges to sand, when to stain the boards, how to assemble the pieces, how many coats of varnish to apply. Will an assembly-line procedure work best? Should I stain outdoors rather than in my shop where space is limited? How long must I wait for the stain and varnish to dry? Should I sand before or after assembly?

Once each step is ordered, I begin the building process. Starting with the first item on the list, I make the preparatory arrangements, clear the work area, schedule my time, obtain the tools I need, buy the lumber. Continuing right down my list, I make the cuts, sand the boards, stain the wood, and assemble the various parts.

In a day or two I have a completed shelf. The picture in my mind has become reality!

Communication at Home

This planning process works in every area of life. Let's say I am having some difficulties in my marriage—my wife and I are no longer communicating our feelings as I think we should. I therefore read a book on marriage, hoping it will give me some insight into my situation.

The author tells me, "At the end of the day when you come home, express an interest in your wife's day. Involve yourself in the small things she has gone through since you left in the morning. Ask her about them; listen to her; feel her day with her. You will soon be communicating."

I read these words and think to myself, "That sounds great! I'd like to communicate with my wife like that."

Already I am visualizing an objective—my wife and I communicating and I becoming a more effective husband. A "faith picture" is coming to life.

I *can* choose to bring this picture into reality. It's entirely up to me (decision!). To do so I must devise a plan. In this case my plan is to follow the advice of the book exactly as the author recommended it—go home, open the door, and express an interest in my wife's day.

The more detailed my plan the better its chances of success. I may prepare specific questions to ask her ("How are you progressing on that new dress you're making? Did you have a chance to work on it today?"). I may call her in the afternoon just to chat, to see how her day is going and to let her know what time I'll be home. I may stop the car a little ways from home to spend a few moments in prayer, gearing down from the pressures of my day and mentally preparing myself to enter into my wife's frame of reference. All these things are part of the plan that I will devise ahead of time.

Once the goal has been set and the plan determined, I must carry it out. When I climb out of the car and walk into the house, I must do *exactly* what my plan calls for. Day after day, if I put my wife's needs, interests, and activities high on my priority list, our communication will grow. I will become a more effective Christian husband. The picture in my mind will become a reality.

Accomplishment Amidst a Housewife's Daily Pressures

Remember Pat Coleman's need to break free from her one-dimensional life and broaden her realms of expression? With a goal and a specific plan, she can.

Let's assume Pat decided on two things she wanted to achieve—read and play the piano regularly. Now Pat needs specific objectives. She thinks reading one book every two weeks would be a good place to begin. She would like to supplement that reading with daily Bible study as well. She would also like to sharpen her piano skills to the point where she could once again give lessons. She feels a half hour per day of practice would be sufficient to attain that goal.

Already her goals are coming clear—read a book every two weeks and practice piano playing a half hour per day (to prepare for giving piano lessons). Pat Coleman is on her way!

Now arises the question of time and priorities—when will she be able to read and study, play the piano, and fit these activities among her present responsibilities? As she assesses her schedule, Pat realizes she doesn't want to take time for these personal pursuits by sacrificing her time with her children and husband. She wants to extract the time necessary to expand her activities from the presently un-used parts of the day. She invests a good deal of thought an-alyzing her day from top to bottom. She considers the option of reading during the children's naps. However, that time is unpredictable at best. Trying to read while they are up and about would also be impossible—that isn't what she wants anyway. Reading just before bed would be risky, she admits, knowing her usual condition by nine o'clock.

Then she strikes upon an idea. Her husband usually gets up 30 to 45 minutes before she does, while she allows herself to sleep till the last moment before the kids wake up. If she could get up with him, it would be a perfect time to read!

Further thought reveals some wasted early evening time. Right after the kids are in bed, she usually just putters about, trying to gather the energy to tackle the dishes. Half an hour is easily wasted just recovering from the hectic day. But, if she went straight to the piano after all the good-nights, she could practice thirty minutes and end up in far better spirits to face the kitchen. Far from missing the time, she would greatly enjoy it!

Pat is excited with the possibilities of a revamped daily schedule. It will help her accomplish some of her goals and improve her outlook. Now she will procure some needed materials. She arranges for a baby-sitter so that she can go out to buy two piano books at the music shop and four books (one a Bible study and the others of general interest) at the Christian bookstore.

Pat has set well-defined goals. She has formulated an effective plan. She has made a firm decision that she will get up no matter how warm and cozy the bed feels, that she will read books and will play the piano daily, no matter how lethargic she may feel. If Pat carries out her plan, one step at a time, and continues day after day, progressing up her own unique staircase, she will find her days flowing more smoothly.

Six months later, Pat's morning time has expanded to an hour. She and her husband spend the first 15 minutes in praying and discussing important issues in their lives. She reads more books than previously and finds her Bible more "alive" than it has been for years. One morning a week she has several friends in for coffee. While their children play in the backyard, they together conduct an informal Bible study. She gives piano lessons to three youngsters in the neighborhood and just last week her own five-year-old asked if she could take lessons from Mommy too. She now plays the piano once a month during the evening song service. Her relationships with the children have improved noticeably. There seem to be fewer tantrums, and although Pat sees no clear connection, she is certain her new attitude has reduced the tension in the home.

Pat is a new woman—all because she decided to utilize two previously wasted 30-minute chunks of the day!

Changing Vocations in Mid-life

Dave Jenkins' solution for getting out of his rut will be considerably more complex than Pat Coleman's. Dave wants an entirely new direction in life and he knows such a thing does not come quickly.

He sees two basic options: return to school with the long-range goal of going to the mission field, or work toward branching out into his own business. Both possibilities are attractive.

As Dave reads a book on motivation, he realizes that he doesn't have to remain in his present position. (A husband or wife can be crucial at this point—helping the other to *believe* in himself, to step into new, unexplored territory. Mrs. Jenkins can provide the boost to accelerate Dave into realms of great productivity for the Lord.)

So Dave begins thinking more specifically about what he wants to accomplish. He thoroughly discusses the options with his wife and pastor. He explores some business possibilities, looks into real estate school and writes for information on various seminaries and mission boards to see whether he would be eligible. He continues with his job while examining every lead.

After six months Dave senses that God is leading him toward the mission field. He has corresponded with several agencies and one has expressed interest in him . He speaks with the leaders by phone and corresponds further by letter.

Increasingly the circumstances seem to fit together and the Lord's guidance appears unmistakable.

Dave finally makes the decision. He will leave his job and go to Central America as a missionary. His experience at the tire plant will prove invaluable at a mission-sponsored rubber plant being planned for that area. The mission agency is excited about Dave's background and skill; Dave is excited about putting his ability to work for the Lord.

There are, however, many practical obstacles to be overcome. Dave will have to take two additional years of schooling at a local seminary before he will be eligible. This will strain the family finances. He explains the situation to his boss. The conference is successful. His boss (for whom Dave and his wife have been praying for some time), contrary to standard company policy, allows Dave to switch from his foreman's position to a more tedious asignment so that he can work just five hours a day. The drop in pay will squeeze the budget, but the schedule will allow Dave to work while attending to school. His wife takes a part-time job at Sears, and with the two half-incomes, they should get by.

In four years Dave Jenkins and his wife are in Costa Rica. Dave works long hours in the new rubber plant and his wife teaches at the mission school. Their two children live with an aunt in Los Angeles and attend college, working part time to pay their expenses.

New vision has breathed life into the Jenkins household! Dave has never been happier. He is out of his rut and into a purposeful, fulfilling new life.

Guidelines for Planning

Let's examine what each of these people's plans have in common. Why did they succeed? Successful planning involves a number of steps. Apply these guidelines to your planning and you will (if you carry them out) reach your goals.

Take Time to Plan

You can't set goals and plan successfully without a regular time to do so. Planning must become an on-going part of your life. Daily spend 15 to 30 minutes meditating on the Lord's direction and organizing your activities.

Establish Goals and Objectives

You may have in mind to do any number of things: land a new account, take a second honeymoon, remodel your office, buy a new home, find a new job, expand your church's Sunday school enrollment, take your children camping for a week, return to school for a teaching degree, teach yourself to play the clarinet, teach your five-year-old to read, clean out the garage, organize the junk in the attic, or start a business.

Determine your precise objectives (if they seem a bit fuzzy) by brainstorming. Then, narrow down all the ideas that bombard you until clear goals begin to form. What *precisely* do you want to do?

State Objectives Concretely

In order to know if you have reached an objective, you must have previously defined it so clearly that you can say beyond any doubt, "I made it," or, "I didn't make it." State *exactly* what will happen—if there will be an event, a decision, an improvement, a finished product, or whatever. In addition, this must be definite and *measurable*—time of day, month and date, dollars and cents, numbers, percentages, hours, feet and inches, pages, miles, minutes, etc.

As an example, "Have an evangelistic youth rally for the young people in our area" is a virtually useless objective as it stands. Where and when will it be? Who will speak—on what topics? Will there be music? Who will plan it? What is its purpose? Who will direct it? How will it be publicized? What is the desired outcome? Who will come? What will happen when it is over? How much will it cost? Who will pay for it?

What you intend to do and *why* must be defined before you can ever hope to begin.

Consider Intermediate Goals

How will you progress toward your ultimate objective? What must you do in the next day, week, or month to reach the long-range goal? What "landings" do you need to build between the bottom step (now) and the top step. Write these intermediate objectives on a sheet of paper to visualize the progression—one-fourth of the way up, in the middle of the page, and three-fourths of the way to the top. Draw a staircase with labeled "landings" if it will help you picture the process.

Detail Every Step

This is the crucial part of the planning process. You now move backwards from objectives to activities, from end results to actions. Working backwards is the key. Always move back from your goal, asking, "What must be done *before* I can. . . ?"

Write Down the Steps in Order

Activities must be done progressively, one at a time. The order of your list becomes the schedule for your plan. Prioritizing your list involves two questions—which of the two activities is most important? And which of two activities must be done first? One is a judgment of value; the other, of sequence.

Next, rewrite your random list in a clear order. For simple lists you can quickly determine the order simply by numbering the activities according to necessity—placing a 1 beside the first thing to be done, a 2 beside the second, etc. We've all done this with our daily tasks.

For more complex jobs, you might want to place every single activity according to three groups: A = *must* do; B = do after A's are completed; C = Do only after A's and B's are completed.

Whatever your selection process, once you have ordered the sequence of activities, you have a workable plan. You have a complete staircase which will take you from the bottom to the top.

As you go to work, it doesn't necessarily matter if you complete a particular list on a given day. Because you have prioritized with care, you can always be confident that you have taken care of the most important items because they came first on the list. You can simply resume your progress on the following day.

Set Deadlines

Now that you have a plan, you need to schedule your plan—*when* to do everything on the list. You must consider two questions: how long will each activity take? and when is it to be done (day, month, hour, etc.)? You need a timetable with deadlines.

Scheduling not only requires setting deadlines for the *completion*, but also for the *beginning* and for various stages of progress. Too often, the only check on progress comes either at the completion date or shortly before. But that is too late if the work is behind schedule. If you are falling behind, you need to know quickly, deal with the problem, and resume the intended pace toward the target. Deadlines at *both* ends and throughout the process insure that an activity will start, progress, and finish on time.

Evaluate Progress as You Proceed

Planning cannot anticipate every aspect. Planning involves thinking through what you *expect* you will need to do. But as you progress you must constantly evaluate and re-plan, coping with things you weren't able to foresee when you began.

This is why intermediate goals are so vital. They allow you to periodically check your progress. Then, if adjustments are necessary, you have the opportunity to make them. You must, therefore, remain flexible and expect plans to change with time. If you are so bound to a plan that you are unable to move in a better direction, you will not achieve at your fullest potential. When you're prevented from going in one direction, don't be stubborn, just be prepared to go in another direction. Never be without a Plan B.

Evaluate Yourself

1. Can I break down my larger goals into smaller, attainable chunks?
2. I write down the steps toward one of my objectives, in order, then tackle them one at a time.

COMPLETE WORKSHEETS #3 AND #4 AT THE BACK OF THE BOOK. (At this point you can begin to see some dramatic changes in your life. Put those planning sheets to work. You *can* reach your goals!)

7. DO IT

The purpose of this book is to help you get more done. But drawing up plans won't get more done. *Carrying them out will.*

Presumably you have a plan of some kind before you, or you are ready to make one. What next? Where do you go from here? What do you *do* with that piece of paper in your hand?

Very simple. Start at the first element of your plan, and follow the instructions—DO IT.

Then move on to step number two—DO IT.

Step three—DO IT.

Step four—DO IT.

This is the key to unlocking the world of productivity and accomplishment inside you—carrying out your plan a step at a time.

If you follow these principles we've discussed, if you set meaningful goals and devise useful step-by-step plans, if you apply your willpower and self-discipline as you carry out every step of your plan, *the sky's the limit!*

You can accomplish anything you want to achieve!

Part II

HOW TO GET MORE DONE MANAGING OTHERS

8. LEADING OTHERS TOWARD YOUR GOAL

If you try to clean your yard, get a new job or return to school for training, you will be able to do so on your own. But if you have a goal involving accomplishment in wider spheres, and are facing the question, "What is the most effective way of getting this job done?" *other people* usually enter the picture. Though substantial accomplishments may be personal—writing books, changing vocations, paraphrasing a portion of Scripture for your children, reading fifty books this year—many projects require others to assist for lasting achievement.

Much of this will depend on your position. Obviously a pastor, businessman, or committee chairwoman will need to work through other people more than will a housewife or student. Yet, whatever your position, you must learn both to elicit help from others and make skillful use of it. For you will always be dreaming dreams that extend far beyond your limited energy, resources, and time. You must be able to manage people wisely.

You Must Learn to Lead

Getting more done in less time with greater efficiency requires that you learn to multiply your time, resources, and energy. This is done by reproducing your vision in others who can also work toward the fulfillment of your goals. Getting things done through other people is the most basic lesson of skillful management. It is a skill all productive men and women must acquire to attain the lofty goals before them. They must be able to lead.

We usually think of "leadership" in connection with position or dynamic personality. But here we are using the term differently. The person who can lead others toward productive achievement is not dependent on position, personality, title, or status. Rather, he or she is one who has the capacity to get a task accomplished. It matters not whether an appropriate title appears on an office door after one's name or whether one has a magnetic personality. *Results, not labels and personalities, measure leadership.*

Many of you have never thought of yourselves as "managers," yet "management" is nothing more than the ability to employ others to help carry out a task—getting a job done through other people. That's what a leader does. He has a vision—a goal toward which he is moving. Setting that goal can be rather simple. But one's effectiveness in reaching it will depend on his ability to mobilize others to work with him. The wise individual with a big vision in his heart recognizes that he needs people to help him. For some, this will mean a paid staff. For others, it will involve volunteers. For fathers, this will mean working with a wife to accomplish family goals. For mothers, this will mean learning to manage their children skillfully.

Some people stubbornly try to operate single-handedly, but in so doing, they clamp a lid on the potential in themselves which God desires to use. The pastor who insists on doing everything himself, rather than tapping the resources among his emerging lay leadership, will stifle what God could otherwise do in his congregation. The mother who refuses to develop responsibility in her children will stunt their maturation. The manager of a business who cannot hand over certain reins of responsibility to capable subordinates will limit the potential growth of his company. The leader of a weekly women's Bible study group who doggedly lectures from start to finish, without allowing participation or training others to teach, will restrict what God is able to accomplish in the group.

Understand, however, that the productive individual does not turn over responsibility simply so he can sleep and lounge around. No. It is so that he can channel his energies into yet broader areas—setting goals and planning for excursions into new and unexplored regions.

You must maintain a balance between what *you* do and what you train *others* to do. You must discover the most productive ways to spend your own time. Large tasks and ambitious goals will demand much energy for thinking, planning, and evaluating. You will therefore need help with the smaller daily jobs so you can be free to work on strategic aspects which require your personal thought and attention. The greater the responsibility the less you will be able to carry out many of the details yourself.

You Must Provide Structure, Definition, and Direction

If you are the person with the goal, you must provide direction for those under you. Everyone watches and listens for what *you* will say and do. You call the shots; they follow. You can't wait for someone to act, or hope your goal will somehow be achieved without any solid direction. It won't happen. Without determined leadership a group will wander and bog down.

Give Careful Instructions

Once people are committed to your goal, you must provide precise, practical instruction concerning what everyone is to *do*. Businessmen call this a "job description"—a concise written summary of what is expected. Whether or not you need such an official format, it is important that you issue each person some clear instructions about what exactly it is you expect them to do.

This is one of the foundational difficulties found in working with people—communicating precisely. And it is especially difficult to be understood by someone with a perspective different from your own. Therefore, you must carefully consider what you need from a certain individual. Then when you deliver his instructions, they will be clear, precise, and simple.

Even if the "job" is nothing more than putting your oldest daughter in charge of her brother and sister for the evening, there must be no doubt in her mind about what she is to do. You must clarify the extent of her authority. She should also know whom to call in an emergency. Just think of yourself as a businessman preparing his assistant before leaving on a business trip.

Every parent, pastor, committee chairman, businessman, camp counselor, foreman, choir director, and teacher must be skilled in the art of giving instructions that are understood and will be carried out. Such clear instructions provide the subordinate with great security—he knows exactly why the job exists, what his specific duties are, what authority he has and to whom he is accountable. Men, women, and children all need a clear picture of what is expected of them. They want to know what constitutes good performance. They want to know how they're doing. Clear instructions from you, their leader, provide this stability and security.

When giving instructions be mindful of two things. First, make certain the individual understands your goals and his part in bringing them to reality. Second, give him specific guidance for his particular job. This must be highly personalized, for everyone does not work in the same way. Never expect uniformity. You must tailor instructions to suit a person's attitudes, aptitudes, and maturity.

The task of giving good instructions that propel you and your people toward a goal places a heavy responsibility on you. You must think through carefully what you want to achieve through *each* person. There's more to effective leadership than simply handing a person a list of things to do and saying, "Get cracking!"

The Need for Clarity

Many job-oriented difficulties stem from vague, indefinite instructions. Instructions must be intensely practical. They must specify well-defined responsibilities. Read Exodus 25 through 30—God's instructions to the Israelites for the building of the tabernacle, ark, and altars. The amount of detail is staggering! Nothing is left to chance.

People need to hear, "This is where you fit; this is why you're here; this is what you do." Everything you ask someone to do must have significance. In all projects involving people, there are those who lead and those who follow. Wherever lines of authority and specific duties exist, relationships must be clarified. If people do not know where they stand or what is expected, they have no basis for evaluating whether they are making headway and are reaching their goals.

Involve People in the Formulation of Their Own Responsibilities

The more one has had a voice in the establishment of standards and responsibilities, the more he will be motivated to meet them. Some parents of teenagers skillfully employ this principle and thus avoid conflict over rules. Discussing the factors and arriving at a mutual decision spares everyone a good deal of grief later on.

If you are a businessman, for example, you can allow the high level employee (under your direction) to structure the specific means he will use to fulfill his job. You probably won't do this with new people, but the longer someone has been with you and the more he has contributed toward your goals, the more latitude he deserves. In the same way a parent will give a sixteen-year-old much greater freedom than he will a five-year-old.

Whenever you issue instructions of any kind, especially regarding the nature of the person's responsibilities, you should encourage suggestions and questions to clarify doubtful or unclear points. This is not time for your employee, assistant, co-worker, or child to "talk down" your expectations and bargain for an easier time of it. We cannot equate negotiation and discussion with haggling for a less-demanding job. The objective here is a clear understanding of a person's responsibilities. You are not trying to change the job itself, but rather, making certain you both understand the specifics of the assignment so that you can both commit yourselves to carrying it out.

Accountability

In providing direction and giving instructions to a subordinate, you must firmly establish several things:
1. *Responsibilities*—what he will *do*.
2. *Authority*—who he will take orders *from* and give orders *to*.
3. *Accountability*—how he will be held responsible for his job.

A key to dynamic progress is that of making people *willing* to assume responsibility for those things within their control. Accepting personal accountability is unpopular. Scapegoats exist for every societal problem and personal hangup. People easily succumb to the temptation to pass blame for everything negative onto someone else's shoulders. Countless times I have heard my own children say, "But I didn't do it—he did!" Though we love to take credit when things go right, we don't like to take the blame and accept the consequences when things go wrong.

Even from the opening pages of the Bible, God has held man accountable for his actions. Though Adam tried to pass the buck to Eve, and Eve tried to pass it onto the serpent, each had to bear the responsibility for his own deeds.

In leadership and management, accountability means shouldering responsibility not only for one's own actions, but also for those things which are under your authority, whether or not you had anything directly to do with it. If it happens *under* you, you are responsible. Adam had to shoulder responsibility for Eve's mistake. If your son breaks a neighbor's window with a foul ball, the neighbors consider it *your* responsibility. (Of course you may then have to hold your son accountable with respect to *his* mistake, but there is no way you can remove yourself from the situation.) If someone on your committe exceeds the authority he was given, *you*, the chairman, must provide a solution.

This is an important principle for the leader in Christian work. For God holds His leaders more accountable than their followers. The higher one goes the greater his responsibility. The greater his responsibility, the greater his accountability. In Numbers 20 Moses makes what appears to be just a minor mistake—he struck the rock instead of speaking to it. Yet because of his position he could not be excused for even a momentary lapse in self-control—"To whom much is given, much is required" (Luke 12:48).

Excessive talk about *why* such-and-such didn't get done—excuses, explanations, justifications—reveals a basic flaw. The responsible person doesn't talk about *why* something wasn't done; he does it. The degree to which a person accepts accountability is a good indication of his efficiency.

I make clear in our store's policy manual: "Just the fact that you work here makes you responsible. If you notice that something isn't as it should be, whether or not it is part of your specific job, in that moment you *become* the person accountable for righting that condition. If you personally cannot take care of it, then get someone who can. But do not walk by thinking, 'That's not my job.' "

My wife and I are trying to develop that sense of accountability in our children. If a rustable toy is outside late in the day and Robin happens to be near it as we are gathering things to bring inside, Judy may say to him, "Robin, will you please bring in that yellow ditch-digger over by the rock pile?"

Usually the response is, "But Patrick brought it out!"

And he may be right. But accountability extends beyond the strict confines of "Who did it?" to "What needs to be done to right the situation?" Therefore, as a member of our family, Robin must learn to accept responsibility for more than what he alone has done.

When a group of people are involved together in a church, business, Sunday school, or volunteer agency, responsibility must emanate from the top downward. There must be a framework of accountability which rests the full weight of what is being done upon those in charge. As a productive person, this must be your perspective—*that you are the most accountable of all.* If you have taken upon yourself to reach some goal and have gathered people to help you in that task, then you must not shirk responsibility but shoulder it squarely.

Supervision

Your objective is to get something done. If people are working with you, then you must have some means of evaluating whether or not responsibilities are being carried out. If things are not being done and your plan is off-schedule, you need to know this so you can make corrections.

Such supervision begins with the instructions themselves. You must have given a person a specific answer to the question, "What must I actually do?" You must always try to communicate that specific duties contribute to the larger objectives toward which you are all working. He needs to know how his job helps fulfill the long-range objectives.

Distant goals must be concrete and obviously related to daily responsibilities. I stress repeatedly to my clerks that dusting, vacuuming, and straightening are vital to maintaining a clean store. In such a pleasant atmosphere, people can be ministered to. When reminding a part-time employee to change the faded books in the window display, I try always to remind her of our purpose. I relate specific instructions to larger goals.

This also can work in the family. Asking my six-year-old son to pick up his room will be more successful if I excite him about the fact that Grandma and Grandpa are coming tonight.

Once clear instructions have been given, you must clarify how the person's work will be evaluated and the degree to which he will be held accountable for his assignment. ("I'll need that report on last year's Sunday school enrollment by next Sunday. I'll call you on Friday night to see how it's coming along and whether it will be finished on time.")

You must make clear who will supervise the work and how often, what the standards are for acceptable performance, what corrective measures he can expect, etc. If you must later confront the person with those aspects of his work which don't measure up, he should not be surprised. He should have known ahead of time what was expected, and how he would be supervised.

If instructions are to be binding, they must be clear. If you want a person to clean the bathroom, tell him, "Please clean the bathroom. Sweep and mop the floor, fill the paper-towel dispensers, and make sure there are two rolls of toilet paper." Don't say, "We've lately been having trouble keeping the towel dispenser full and there have been some complaints about the bathroom floor being dirty. We really ought to check it a little more often. Do you suppose you might look into that when you have the chance?"

You will *think* you told him to clean the bathroom, but he will never have heard anything of the sort.

When giving instructions, use short words and sentences. Be brief. Stick to one idea per sentence. Don't ramble into lengthy explanations about *why* everything must be done. Stick to *what* is to be done with just enough *why* so the significance of the job is clear.

If giving oral instructions, have them repeated back to you. Always check to make sure what is heard corresponds with what you wanted to say. ("Johnny, please go to the store and buy a dozen eggs, a gallon of milk, and a loaf of bread. Now, Johnny, tell me what you are going to buy.")

Clear agreement about what has been said is absolutely essential. You cannot hold a person accountable for something he was never told to do. This principle applies universally—to the corporate president, to the pastor, to the mother of a five-year-old.

With this groundwork laid in advance, you are able to evaluate performance. If you have been clear, then what has been done either does or does not meet the standard. Johnny either bought the bread, milk, and eggs or he did not. If he forgot the eggs, then you as his parent have the reasonable duty to hold him accountable.

Authority

The final thing you must clarify in the minds of those who work with you concerns their working relationships. They are responsible *to whom* and *for what*.

Relationships extend in three directions: up, down, and sideways. A person must know who his superior is and what the relationship entails—up. He must also understand the nature of his authority over his subordinates—down. Finally, he must be clear about those other people who work on either side of him—sideways. ("I take my orders from this man; I oversee the work of these people; I can consult with this woman, but she doesn't issue me direct instructions. There is also another department and committee over there that is exercising a related, yet distinct responsibility of its own.")

This principle is of paramount importance in every family and church. The degree to which lines of authority are understood is a good indication of the harmony that will exist.

Think Through Assignments Ahead of Time

Providing wise leadership through precise instructions takes time and energy. If you try to prepare job descriptions quickly, they will do you and your fellow workers little good. But if you put thought, prayer, and planning into them, they will save hours in the future. By analyzing what you want done in advance you save having to re-think it all later. If your planning is skillful and everyone is clear about his responsibilities, you can watch your church, ministry, study group, business, family, or volunteer group run smoothly.

These Are Universal Principles

At the very beginning of this book I warned you that some of what we would discuss would sound distinctly "businesslike." This chapter has probably been the most businesslike of all. If you are a businessman or a pastor or some other kind of leader in charge of many people, you will have no trouble applying these principles.

But what about the rest of you? Have you had some difficulty seeing how all this talk of "leading" could apply in your situation?

If so, I encourage you to re-read this section. After each

point ask yourself how this could apply to those people you deal with. Force yourself into some application and you'll begin to discover countless ways to improve your relationships. We see these principles coming to life daily, right in our family in our relationship with our boys.

With a little work you'll discover them making a difference in your life as well.

Evaluate Yourself

1. Do I consider myself a leader? How would I rate my leadership effectiveness? In what areas am I presently responsible to lead?
2. Am I definite and clear when I communicate? In what ways am I often misunderstood?
3. In my working relationships, are the lines of accountability spelled out? Is the supervision process working?

9. DELEGATION—RAISING UP TOMORROW'S LEADERS

No matter how lofty and magnificent our objectives, we must never forget we are part of an even larger purpose— God's plan for His people. We therefore have a deep responsibility to God's children who will follow on after us. We are charged with training and preparing them for the ministries to which God will call them.

Christian leadership involves discipling. The productive person is observed and emulated. Being a godly example is one of his prime functions.

Discipling requires training. A leader must prepare those under him for accomplishments of their own by carefully placing them into circumstances which stretch and develop their capabilities.

This process of discipling is seen frequently in the Scriptures. Moses had his Joshua, Elijah his Elisha, and Jesus His twelve. Paul's relationship with Timothy was clearly one of gradually building leadership skills into him. Timothy's gifts were carefully nurtured and brought to the surface by his wise and experienced mentor. In the same way, effective pastors disciple their laymen, and effective parents disciple their children.

Delegation, an important aspect of discipling, means to assign a task which is not part of a person's normal routine. A pastor, for example, occasionally delegates the preaching of a sermon to one of his lay leaders. It is the pastor's responsibility, but he has assigned it to another for the training it provides. Similarly, a mother will occasionally give her daughter responsibility for the evening meal. This is part of her long-range plan to teach her homemaking skills. Cooking is the mother's job but she assigns it to her daughter to build confidence. A choir director may hand over the rehearsal of a certain anthem and its performance to someone he feels has directing potential. A Bible study leader may sometimes assign a week's lesson to another, thus allowing him to test the waters of leadership. Delegation is entrusting another with a specific assignment and then providing the training he needs to carry it out effectively.

Though delegation often involves one-time assignments (which may be repeated a number of times), there is nothing haphazard about it. One does not delegate some unsavory aspect of his job to any person who happens to be around just to get out of doing it. (Blurting, "Here, take care of this. . . ," as you hasten out the door, is not skillful delegation.)

Delegation is a well-planned process. You must have an individual plan for each person and be committed to helping each attain his maximum potential. You gradually add to a person's responsibilities and authority. When he performs well and gains your confidence, you can turn more over to him. Far from being a means to get a particular job crossed off your list, delegation is the application of your specific vision for each person under you.

Anyone moving upward into responsibility needs to gradually test new waters beyond his present position. You must temporarily place more on his shoulders than he is accustomed to. The challenge will stimulate him to new heights of confidence and will widen his horizons. It will give him the chance to show what he can do and learn where his weaknesses are. It thus prepares him to later move into these realms permanently. Someone from whom nothing is expected beyond present tasks will never learn to make decisions. He won't have the opportunity to develop latent skills. He will prove himself unfit for leadership, due to sheer lack of practice.

Delegation Provides Needed Assistance

Though raising up your people is the motive for delegation, it has a practical side benefit. Delegation increases your available time by distributing your workload. If your vision is growing as it should, you are responsible for more than you can possibly handle. That's the nature of leadership. From a pragmatic standpoint, you need help! Delegation, therefore, not only trains others, it frees you to do other things.

Many suffer from the if-only-I-worked-fifteen-hours-a-day-I'd-get-everything-done logic. But it doesn't work. Your responsibilities will continue to increase. The key to getting more done does not lie in longer hours.

But you mustn't wait until you're snowed under to delegate. By then it's too late to give the process adequate planning. You will be tempted to pass along duties to others simply to relax your own load. You must incorporate into your ongoing system a method of gradually eliminating lower responsibilities to make room for the new ones coming your way. Not because the lower ones are unimportant, but because they are things others can be trained to do.

Your whole group can thus grow simultaneously. As a person repeatedly performs delegated tasks well, certain of these new tasks can be integrated into his permanent responsibilities. You must always be working yourself out of a job, looking for those areas of *your* job you can train *someone else* to do. This is necessary both for your subordinate's growth and for your own. As you let go of one rung of the ladder you take hold of a higher rung. As you give your subordinate new assignments, some of his previous functions will have to be passed along to someone else. It is a continual process. The very nature of growth requires it.

You the leader must give purpose and structure to this process. Delegation is not a fancy name for passing the buck. It is a tool to free you for high priority items and to give your people useful experience. The first time around, the job will take longer than if you had done it yourself. But once that person's skill increases, you'll reap the dividends of your investment.

Delegation can be difficult. It's hard to release control. We become paralyzed by the I'm-the-only-one-around-who-can-do-it mentality (which actually means you lack confidence in your training process). But you will impede the growth of your vision if you refuse to let go of certain tasks.

As a productive person, you must be a multiplier. Your concentration is too important to be continually diluted with details that can be handled by another. You must have time to think, plan, and evaluate. If your day is consumed with small matters (possibly crucial but that others can deal with), your effectiveness is dramatically reduced. You must know when to delegate details. You must concentrate on strategic matters.

You must realize (painfully at first) that if your organization is to be efficient and reach its objectives, you cannot have your fingers in every pie. You can't be in touch with every detail. Many small family businesses never grow because one person single-handedly tries to handle every activity. Churches never grow for the same reason.

When asked about the key to his success, Andrew Carnegie once replied, "I am merely a man who knows how to enlist in his service better men than himself."

The one-man show can't get very far off the ground. Knock the ceiling off your potential and GO where the Lord wants you to. Be willing to let go.

Moses—An Example of Delegation

Moses was responsible for leading over two million

people out of Egypt to Canaan. From morning till night he found himself besieged by people needing counsel, decision, and judgment. His days were consumed making these decisions, case-by-case. He did very little management (using others) and had no time to seek God's direction for the people.

In Exodus 18 his father-in-law Jethro observed what was going on. He came to Moses and said, "Moses, this job's too big for you. You've got to get some help. Delegate some of this to capable men who can share the load."

Moses humbly heeded his advise and set the delegation process in motion. He chose and trained men, making sure they were familiar with God's laws and would faithfully represent the leadership he was responsible to provide. He did not just turn them loose.

The whole structure for leading this vast throng was tranformed. Leaders were placed over thousands, hundreds, fifties, and tens. Then seventy men were chosen to share with Moses "the burden of the people." There was both job-sharing and burden-sharing. The changes not only freed Moses from the crushing demands but also prepared Israel's future leaders. When Moses died forty years later, there was no interruption in progress toward the land of promise. Leaders were ready to carry on after him.

Delegation Principles

As you delegate you develop an individual at a predetermined pace you have established. You must have assessed what he can handle and when.

Delegation means little without corresponding freedom within the boundaries you establish. Spell out the latitude you are giving your subordinate, then let him go. Allow him even to experiment.

He needs freedom to make mistakes without your continual over-the-shoulder inspection. You're not relinquishing the reins by doing this, just loosening them. You obviously do not wait for a catastrophe before stepping in with assistance. The first time around you may have to help throughout the entire project, but you must be always stepping back to give elbow room.

Delegation is most successful when a person is challenged. Open the way for initiative and ingenuity. This can be achieved by giving him something significant to accomplish, a problem to solve. Make clear what the limitations are and what resources are available, but do not tell him what to do or how to do it. Let him figure it out. Make clear the results you are after, but leave the "how" to him.

I use this technique constantly in our store: "Joni, we need a Thanksgiving window display and I'd like you to set it up. Here are some dried leaves and gourds for background color. Emphasize books for fall and Christmas. There's poster board in the back room. Now show us that creativity that is inside you just waiting to burst forth!" Sometimes I give more instruction, sometimes less. When a person discovers his latent gifts in this way, his enthusiasm ignites.

Evaluate and discuss the successes and failures once the job is completed. When an individual has been responsible for a decision he will be more inclined to scrutinize what he has done, discover mistakes, and make future improvements. His accountability, however, should be lower, since at this point, you are more interested in training than in actual output. Correction is not necessary here, but mutual discovery of how things can be improved is. He needs low-pressure guidance and feedback.

Building confidence is a part of successful delegation. Rather than criticism, there needs to be a healthy what-can-we-learn-from-this-experience approach to mistakes. As your subordinate explores new areas he must feel your enthusiasm for his efforts. He must sense your confidence. He will thrive on being trusted. Let him learn from personal exposure. Most men and women are capable of far more than they are presently doing. They just need self-assurance to bring their dormant skills to the surface.

There is a dangerous tendency either to turn our backs completely or else step in and solve every minor problem. But we must balance the two—give direction, then stand back, step in as needed, then back off again. The person develops initiative and resourcefulness when forced to think through problems. Coach, don't boss at this point. People need to be shown what they did *right*.

Allow the person to revel in his successes. Even your minor criticisms should ring with appreciation and praise because he tried something new. When the new responsibility is finally added to his permanent job, this will change. Then you will expect high performance. But when delegating extra assignments, you must show appreciation for every effort.

How to Begin

The first full-time worker I hired for our store was a clerk. As I became aware of his competence, I occasionally delegated orders to him, while I retained control of the general ordering process. He performed well. I therefore continued to give him specific ordering assignments, always discussing with him additional aspects of the ordering routine. Gradually I gave him more complex tasks, including the monthly inventory of our stock on which orders are based.

It would have been too drastic to simply tell him one day, "Do the ordering." So I continued to handle the bulk of it, but gradually handed over the responsibility to him. His skill continued to increase as did the extent of his duties.

After about a year he was doing all the ordering. I had indeed worked myself out of that job.

The delegation process did not stop there. He began to assist in training other workers and in keeping record of accounts payable and receivable. He helped me develop an inventory control system which became the subject for a book we wrote, published, and distributed. After a two-year process of training him through delegation, he became my assistant manager. He is today responsible for a majority of the day-to-day management of the store.

I have further plans for his growth. I continue to develop him in new areas. And at the same time I encourage him to delegate some of his duties to those under him. He has now entrusted portions of the monthly inventory check to others, making room in his schedule for the higher things that are continually coming his way.

And what has this process done for our business? Five years ago we had one store—basically a one-man operation. That man was *me*. But because I have delegated most of the work I am free to concentrate on things other than details. There are now four large stores, doing six times the volume of business we were doing then. Not only have we grown, the process has been valuable for those involved—such as my assistant. He is today a wise businessman whom I trust and respect. I couldn't survive without him. We continue to delegate work to our people to help them develop—to distribute the workload, and to enhance the future of our business.

Evaluate Yourself

1. Am I discipling and developing my people and encouraging them to grow?
2. In what responsibilities am I swamped? Could delegation ease my load as well as develop someone else?

10. MOTIVATION—GETTING OTHERS TO DO MORE

To lead effectively you must become a motivator. You can make effective co-workers and build future leaders only as you spark within them a personalized sense of your vision and objectives. This you can do in a number of ways.

Build Upon Natural Needs and Aspirations

The effective leader will know an individual's needs and aspirations and will seek to fulfill them. This is the essence of motivating.

We all have a fire burning within—a desire to succeed and be recognized for our accomplishments. If you want your subordinate to be fulfilled by his responsibilities, you must know him as a unique individual. What gives him a feeling of self-worth? How can you help him feel significant? How can his job provide him with greater fulfillment? What are his family needs? What are some of his personal goals? If he is employed by you, what responsibility have you taken upon yourself for his financial condition?

Unless your workers can see that you are interested in the details of their lives, they will sense they are merely cogs in a machine. Enthusiasm will be nil, accomplishment low.

Everyone not only has needs but aspirations. The leader must become aware of these secret goals, and then help to reach them. He must structure *his* goals to become *theirs*. Provide incentive by enriching your people's job with greater responsibilities, challenges, and rewards. People require stimulation.

115

Trust Your People

Growth and self-motivation flourish in a climate of trust, positive rapport, and mutual respect. Though you may occasionally have to crack the whip, a spirit of camaraderie must be woven into the fabric of your relationships. This will demonstrate itself in small ways. Words of criticism or anger will not fall carelessly from your lips. You will not upbraid one person in front of another. You will not embarrass or ridicule. You will be honest. You will treat others' ideas with respect. Your manner will communicate, "I trust you. You are important and valuable to me. I'm glad we're on the same team."

Visualize People in Terms of Their Potential

Were God to look upon us as we *are,* it would be impossible for Him to use any of us. God is able to make something of us because He sees us in terms of what we are becoming. This is how you can develop those under you—by visualizing their potential. How you perceive a man or woman determines how he will function. A man who knows you have confidence in him will be motivated to produce.

A primary function of the Christian leader is to develop the many gifts lying dormant in his people and to awaken each to his hidden assets. Though he cannot *cause* potential to be realized, he can take an active hand in the process. He must structure opportunities. He can provide atmosphere for development.

You must be on the lookout for potential and then draw it to the surface. Be aware that God has made each individual a gifted person with significant things to accomplish. He may outperform you in the end! What an opportunity has been placed in your hands! Give him a new vision of himself, a vision that will lift him to new heights.

Your subordinate is less likely to see his gifts than you

are. Give him a vision of himself and you will unlock his way to a significant and fruitful future.

Throughout the Bible are examples of great men raised up under the guidance of another. Consider the Lord's word to Moses in Deuteronomy 3:28 concerning his disciple: "Give Joshua his commission, encourage him and strengthen him; for he will lead this people across, and he will put them in possession of the land you see before you" (NEB).

The Lord's charge to Moses is also fitting for us if we are raising people to the potential He has for them:

1. *Commission them*—Give them a vision.
2. *Encourage them*—Support, and affirm and trust them, giving them wise, deserved praise.
3. *Strengthen them*—Gradually force them into new areas in which they will gain confidence and valuable experience.

Lead by Example

Allow your workers to take initiative, to make decisions. Challenge them—don't let them settle for ten if they are capable of fifteen.

As this process unfolds, they need to see *you* in action. You are the model. Let your character, your enthusiasm, your goals and vision rub off. If you are training someone to witness, take him someplace and let him see you do it. What you *are* will have greater impact than what you *say*. *You* are the model.

You can delegate because you have worked your way up through the delegated tasks yourself. I can delegate a window display because I have created dozens of window displays myself. The manager unwilling to get down on his hands and knees and scrub the floor will discover a dimension of his leadership missing. A pastor who spends more time in his study than out among his flock will prove an ineffective model. He will not build compassionate relationships as examples to those men in his congregation he is trying to disciple. They will eventually practice a similar ivory-tower leadership. A leader must be a servant. Example is a prime motivator, a driving force behind effective leadership.

Plan for Success

Nothing shatters motivation quicker than a know-it-all response to an excited young protégé's new idea—"Oh, yeah, we tried that three years ago. It didn't work."

But enthusiasm breeds motivation. If someone has a poor idea or a pointless comment, you don't need to tell him so. If you can show enthusiasm, even toward poor ideas, your people will get charged up enough to work the bugs out on their own.

Once you have given a person responsibility he *must* succeed, so make sure the task contains a significant level of success. Your response, more than the level of output, will determine this. Nothing will get a person to go all out like the words, "Wow! I'm really proud of you! Terrific job!"

This principle of motivation baffles our logical minds. The more enthusiasm we generate the more a person will be motivated to attain even greater successes and to discover the flaws in his technique. He will grow more quickly through compliments than through criticism of every detail that is wrong. Praise will encourage ingenuity, challenge creativity, and build resourcefulness.

If I "come unglued" over something one of my boys has done, I exclaim, "Fantastic! Did *you* think of that all by yourself? Wow!"

He then runs off charged up for even greater achievements! In no time he has made great strides forward and many improvements.

But if I say, "That's not bad, but look how much better

it would be if this were . . . and if you did this . . . and this isn't quite right. . . ," he turns and slowly walks away, possibly never to try it again.

Success motivates. Criticism disheartens.

A worker gauges his success by the response, *not* the result. We make a child, or a co-worker, successful by our praise. The actual result is secondary. In the moments following the completion of some project, he is still running on the emotional energy generated by the feeling of accomplishment. This is no time to burst his balloon with a critical word. There will be plenty of time for detailed analysis later, if needed. In the quiet of the office the two of you can analyze the whole thing, learning all you can from the experience.

Mark Twain once remarked, "I can live for at least a month on one good compliment." That's human nature. We thrive when we feel good about what we have done, and we will try again. Every attempt will come closer to perfection. That's why critical analysis is not nearly so important as praise.

The skillful parent or teacher is not anxious to say to the child, "Blue and yellow make green." She is content to bide her time, praise all efforts and thereby keep interest high. Finally one day she hears from the next room, "Hey! Mom! I just mixed the blue and yellow paints and. . . ."

Certainly the negative aspects may eventually have to be dealt with. But those must remain secondary for now. You are concerned with *potential* at this point, not the cold statistical facts of the result. That is why it is better to stimulate another's *own* thoughts in new areas than to give lectures about all you know. Let him learn for himself. The test of your leadership skills is not in what *you* know. You have years of experience and are a leader because you know more than your subordinates. That is assumed. The true test is if you can successfully motivate another to discover—*on his own*. What *he* does is the test of your leadership, not what *you* can do. Though perhaps the first results may be minimal, the very fact that they are *his* results makes them monumental. This is not to say every little detail is lauded superficially. Learn the art of giving *meaningful* praise.

Communicate Clearly

Foggy communication leads to misunderstanding. It can bring all sorts of trouble. Effective leaders must learn to communicate with their people.

The most important element in good communication is clarity of expression. *Say what you mean!* Be clear and precise, straight to the point. If you level with your people and mince no words, they will not only understand you, they will also respect and trust you.

This doesn't mean not to guard your words. You must choose what to say and when to say it. But when you do speak, your praise is genuine, your criticisms are meant to help. Be tactful and courteous, but do not obscure what you have to say.

This means more than being honest. It means being *definite*—clear, concise, distinct. It is possible to be honest and yet leave issues clouded. I have corrected employees only to realize later they didn't even know I was calling for improvement. I had been honest, but my method of expression had been so vague I was completely misunderstood.

We often say with 1,000 words what could be said with 100. Don't say any more than is necessary. Use crisp words, simple sentences, logical arguments. Make a statement without having to lead up to it, soften it, justify it, or explain it. Don't automatically assume you've been understood. Ask to have instructions repeated back. Then follow up with a memo or some other kind of check to discover whether things have been done appropriately.

Communication is two-sided. To communicate *to* your

people you must receive communication *from* them. You must listen. Most people are self-oriented and have difficulty focusing on someone else's ideas. We are so absorbed in our own view points that our minds are whirling with our own thoughts—even when we are supposedly listening. As leaders we must overcome this tendency. We must orient our minds toward the *other* person. We must be known as someone who will listen to grievances and new ideas. Our ears must be tuned to the wavelengths of those around us. Learn to listen not just to words but to what is being *felt*. Don't listen through your biases and emotional responses, but through *theirs*.

Communication involves much more than what we say and how we say it. It involves our entire relationship with another individual. Communication is feeling his heartbeat. It is building a bridge to the *real* him. Communication will occur to the extent of your caring. Listen, be patient, ask personal questions, put yourself in his position and say things in love.

Openness

The most dynamic and productive people are receptive to the people and ideas about them. When confronted with something that hasn't crossed their path of experience, their response is, "What can I learn from this?" Such a leader is on the growing edge of life—forward-looking, learning, maturing.

Sadly, a huge percentage of Christians, including their leaders, respond in the opposite manner. They give ready answers to challenges on the basis of their own limited experiences. "*This* is what I have seen, *this* is what I believe, *this* is how God has worked in my life, *this* is how God has worked in our church— therefore I see no reason to change." They refuse to question their idolized viewpoints and expect all Christians to see things exactly as they do. They thus short-circuit much of what God could do in their lives and through their churches.

The leader God can use must be flexible. He must see God at work outside his *own* perception of truth, outside his *own* circle, outside his *own* experience, outside his *own* interpretation of scripture. This requires humility and a hunger to learn and grow. Rather than feeling threatened by "other" viewpoints and experiences, the flexible person is challenged by these evidences of the expansiveness of God's work among men.

Such a person can motivate others because he has an outlook that is *wide open*. He seeks truth from whatever source it may come. He is eager to be enriched. He associates and interacts with a variety of people and ideas. He knows he has much to learn. He guards his mind from stagnation, from the I-won't-consider-anything-I'm-not-already-familiar-with mentality. Therefore, he never stops thinking. He always explores, listens, and seeks to understand.

If this open-minded, vigorous mentality is lost, one's spiritual ears and eyes grow clogged and dull. The capacity to lead is lost.

The Secrets of Motivation

1. Involve each person in planning and goal setting and thus maintain high interest. If someone has a hand in structuring policy, he will work hard to make it succeed. If, however, all decisions are handed down with an impersonal, "Do it," the motivation to jump in excitedly just isn't there.

2. Make him see that completing the task will benefit *him*. All motivation stems from *wanting* to do something. An order won't necessarily bring it about.

3. Make the person think he originated the idea. If he comes up with the idea on his own, though it may have taken some prodding and stimulation on your part, he will be

more likely to follow through on it. When appropriate, skillfully disguise some of your orders as suggestions or requests.

4. Challenge a person to compete against others to gain better results. Give him causes to fight for clear goals that provide emotional rallying points. Then cheer him on and reward accomplishment.

5. Help him set his own goals.

6. Whenever possible, allow a person to work in his own way. Let him try to improve methods.

7. Unless you need a more direct approach, skillfully call attention to minor mistakes indirectly. Motivate a person to remedy inefficiencies on his own so you aren't always the heavy criticizer. Say, "This is an interesting problem—what happened?" rather than the heavy-handed, "You blew it!" Avoid backing a person into a corner and forcing him to be defensive.

8. Send an individual on a mission as your personal trouble-shooter.

9. Encourage new and fresh ideas. When they are offered, receive them enthusiastically. Try as many of the ideas as you can. Let a person experiment with his own ideas.

10. Treat a person's work as valuable. Help him feel a sense of accomplishment in everything he does.

11. Make sure you know an individual's goals. Then spare no effort to meet them. Someone has said, "Find a man's button, then punch it!" We all respond to those things which help us achieve our personal goals. Get on *his* wavelength; don't expect him to be on *yours*.

Evaluate Yourself

1. Do I know what makes my people tick? What gives them a feeling of accomplishment?
2. To what extent am I able to trust others?
3. Can I visualize potential? Do I have a personal vision for

each person working under me?

4. Do I communicate my confidence in others? Do I praise freely? Am I an interested listener?

5. Am I willing to let the "real me" show? How do I respond to ideas outside the scope of my experience?

Part III

FINDING OUT WHAT WENT WRONG

11. DISCOVER AND DEAL WITH INEFFICIENCIES

What looks good on paper doesn't always work out in reality. Unknowns throw the best of plans off course. You won't always accomplish everything you had hoped to. Work will take longer than planned, inefficiencies will creep in.

In the early stages of a project it's impossible to foresee all the potential problems. Therefore, you must continually evaluate and anticipate. You must plan regular checkpoints which allow you to review your progress.

Evaluation and problem-solving are not a last resort after things have gone wrong. They must be an essential component of your project.

This is because the tendency of even the most dedicated persons is to move in independent, uncoordinated directions. Men follow the dictates of their own inclinations. Carrying out a plan involving people resembles a cattle drive. Cattle constantly wander from the herd; they must be brought back and redirected forward by the horseman controlling their progress. Our control must extend not only to those aspects of a plan which won't work, but also to those which wander into ineffectiveness. We must rein them in tightly and remind them, "We're going in *this* direction."

We are reluctant to evaluate progress; to succeed in a task we must continually monitor activities and be alert to problems. The most difficult part of the control process is deciding what specifically is to be done. The successful leader is willing to tackle problems head-on. If something is standing in the way of the plan, he deals with it.

Ambiguity causes much frustration, particularly in Christian churches and organizations. We must not hesitate to use specific words. For instance, if you assign someone to open mail, an effective standard needs to accompany that responsibility. The person must know beyond any doubt if he has performed adequately. "Open all mail on the day received. File invoices and statements. Throw away junk mail. Send out all necessary replies by the evening of the same day." The order, "Efficiently process mail," isn't enough. Use exact words so that if, on a given morning, the previous day's mail lies unopened on the desk, there is no doubt—the standard has not been met.

Clear standards of required performance leave no room for the tendency in Christian ministries to spiritualize a task. In Christian work too frequently there is no *must*: I *must* read an hour today, I *must* prepare for this meeting, I *must* write that letter today, I *must* get up at six, I *must* process this mail before five, I *must* do this job precisely according to these standards.

It's easy to be lazy. We balk at holding ourselves and our people accountable, at measuring performance and expecting conformity to specific standards. It's far simpler to allow standards to grow fuzzy. Therefore we lack discipline in our own lives. We don't enforce a *must* for ourselves, either.

But if you have committed yourself to do something important, you *must* do it. If someone agrees to do something as part of a church program, you as his leader are to measure whether or not he did it. If the job turns out to be unimportant, eliminate it. But if the person has a valid responsibility he must carry it out. You can't just say, "I'll leave the specific outcome between you and the Lord." That's just another way of saying, "I haven't set any definite standards so you won't have to carry out the assignment according to any precise terms." This sort of stance makes effective evaluation impossible.

Your concern is to accomplish that which the Lord has laid on your heart. Therefore, you must have standards that measure success—vacuum the floor daily by 10 a.m.; send out all the day's correspondence by 5:30 p.m.; have a preliminary budget on my desk by the 17th; contact potential spring and summer speakers for the church women's club by February 8, at 5 p.m.; present me with a rough draft by the day after tomorrow at 11 a.m. of a letter to be sent to the local churches about the June family seminar.

Specific Evaluation

Progress can be evaluated in several ways. The method you use in each circumstance will depend on the standards. A statistical report is the simplest to get and the simplest to compare with quantitative objectives: The goal was to have $250 by the 7th; today is the 5th and we have $189.

That is a clear-cut statistical summary. Now you can discuss what options are open for obtaining the necessary $61 within the next two days. What changes in the original plan have to be made? What is "Plan B" if the money is *not* raised?

Many types of activities and assignments can be evaluated statistically. For instance, if you enlist a new teacher in your Sunday school, do not simply hand her the material she will use. It is not even enough (although better) to say, "Look this over. If you have any questions, call me."

Present to her, instead, specific standards. Say, "Here is your material. By the 25th of this month give me an outline of your lesson plans for your first four Sundays. Detail what activities will take place, the time they will take, and how they will be coordinated with this material. We'll discuss your plan, and if you seem to be sufficiently prepared, you will begin teaching on the 4th of next month." You have given a date and a specific standard—a four-week detailed outline—by which you can measure progress. Either it will be done or it won't.

Of course, the person's outline will not tell you whether he is a competent teacher. Further evaluation will be needed to determine that. Other factors such as attendance, discipline, communicating ability, rapport with the children, and cooperation with other teachers will have to be considered.

More subjective means will often be necessary to evaluate less-definable objectives. If a person is not progressing as he should it can be helpful to ask him to write an assessment of the situation and possible reasons for the delay. This provides a springboard for further discussion.

The most subjective means of all evaluation is personal observation of people in action. You must learn to get a "feel" for what is going on and what is needed by watching, and asking the Holy Spirit for insight. This is especially necessary when you are judging elusive qualities perhaps unsuited to a measurable standard—such qualities as morale, commitment, relationships, personal growth. Though you must always be seeking measurable ways to assess these things, cut-and-dried reports can rarely reveal attitude difficulties. You need to feel these things at the gut level.

When Judy and I become aware of some problem or new situation in one of our boys' lives, we have to talk about it with each other and with him. We discuss our observations and sift through possible causes and solutions. It's very subjective. After all, how can we "measure" insecurity, jealousy, or anger?

Making Corrections

Isolate the Problem

When you uncover a problem, you must adjust, correct,

or modify as necessary. At such a point you must stop and plan, spending adequate time considering alternatives. Even though such planning may be short in a crisis situation, you must first know the problem so you can determine what to do. What is really wrong? Why did it happen? Get beneath surface symptoms to root causes.

If an individual is doing sloppy work, the first reaction is usually, "He's not doing his job!" But maybe his poor performance is only a symptom of something deeper you must uncover.

Devise a Strategy

Begin to seek potential solutions, to break major problems into manageable chunks that can be tackled one at a time (attack a mountain of a problem, molehill by molehill). You may begin with a simple list of options. You then eliminate the impractical ones, seeking God's guidance as you do. If a solution does not become immediately apparent, you may need to test potential solutions. A trial run might reveal viability. Find everything that is wrong with your planned solution. Discover loopholes in advance. Don't compound difficulties with an untried solution that may only lead to worse problems.

Summon the Courage to Move Ahead

After thorough evaluation you will formulate a plan. Making tough, thorny decisions is the mark of a mature person. It is easy in a knotty dilemma to just wait, do nothing, and hope it will go away. But neglected problems usually do only one thing—get worse!

You've simply got to launch out. After weighing the evidence declare, "Here's what we're going to do." Realize that you will occasionally blow it, but if you expect your work to go forward, make a decision.

The Holy Spirit's guidance is crucial here. But don't be bound by the commom "spiritual" mentality which equates valid decisions with a euphoric sense of God's direct inspirational control. We can be quite free to toss around the phrase, "feeling the leading of the Lord." But when you solve problems, make decisions, and listen to the advice of others, you won't always be able to assert that you made a wholly "God-inspired" decision. Certainly your heart and mind must be open to all He would say. But remember that the greater your role in the Lord's work, the more decisions He is going to leave in *your* hands.

God *will* give encouragement, strength, confirmation, open and closed doors, as well as strong "leadings." But for every decision you won't get special-delivery telegrams detailing the precise course of action you are to take. Much of the time you'll have to make up your own mind. Your decisions will be just that—*your* decisions.

If your thoughts, motives, and activities are submitted to the Lord, you can confidently move forward. Know that He does work *through* your decisions, that His Spirit does prompt you to act according to His will. Even though *you* make the vital choices, you have to walk in the Spirit, trusting God to be working in you.

Remember God's words to Moses: "I will help you speak and will teach you what to do" (Ex. 4:15).

Remember His promise: "Commit to the Lord whatever you do, and your plans will succeed" (Prov. 16:3).

Remember Paul's word to the Philippians: "For it is God who works in you to will and to act according to his good purpose" (Phil. 2:13, NIV).

Trust these promises and you can trust the decisions you make. Judge what is the best thing to do. Decide to do it. Then, in faith, move ahead.

Evaluate Yourself

1. Do I shy away from honest evaluation when things are

going wrong? Do I often find myself ignoring problems, hoping they'll go away?

2. If I have a problem, what is the root of it? I need to isolate the cause!

3. What courses of action might provide a solution to this problem?

12. PEOPLE TEND TO STRAY

Problems will never be overcome automatically. Even if you properly use checkpoints and follow all the procedures, you will still find yourself stymied by impossible circumstances. For there is one factor which will time and again throw you off course; that factor is *people*.

The Nature of Human Nature

Call it what you will—original sin, human nature, laziness, irresponsibility, immaturity, selfishness, nobody-takes-pride-in-their-work-anymore. But the fact is, people tend to stray away from what they're supposed to do. We've all made commitments and wandered from them. Even if a man agrees to do it, even *wants* to do it, he often will not live up to your expectations.

This will prove your biggest frustration as you try to accomplish something through people. This universal tendency is simply the way people are. Therefore, you must get your work done in spite of it.

You can give clear instructions, develop elaborate standards, formulate trememdous goals and a flawless plan, exercise the most thorough evaluation in the world and have a core of enthusiastic people who are dedicated to you 100 percent. But in the end, the nature of human nature is to wander off. Your guidelines and policies and techniques won't change that. But they will provide you a basis for determining when your people get off the track.

It's not a question of *will* they? That's certain. The

reason is found in Isaiah 53:6. It is a clear biblical principle we are all familiar with: "We *all*, like sheep, have gone astray, each of us has turned *to his own way*" (NIV).

Therefore, if you want to get something done with people, you must exercise close supervision.

Close Personal Supervision

If you want a person to do a job, you cannot tell him to do it, then leave him alone. You may come back some time later to exclaim, "Hey, you didn't do it like I said!"

By then it's too late—the letter is typed, the concrete has set, the house is built, the committee is formed, the deadline is past, the money is spent. It's *done*! And if it has been done wrong, everyone pays the price.

You've got to *make sure* it gets done properly. Evaluation will only tell you it hasn't been done according to your standards. That's not enough. You've got to make sure it *gets* done. And that takes personal supervision.

Supervision is one of the keys to accomplishment. Why do you think large corporations set up such long, thorough lines of accountability? Assistant managers supervise the workers, managers control the assistant managers, regional managers oversee the managers, the general manager guides the regional managers, the president directs the general manager, the board of directors keeps track of the president, and stockholders keep a rein on the board of directors. It is because we *all* stray from our commitments. Even responsible men, such as general managers, presidents, pastors, and elders—even you and I.

You can't wind people up, send them off in a direction and expect them to run on a track faithfully, doing their jobs flawlessly year after year. Humans tend to act selfishly, complain, behave compulsively, act unwisely, rebel, criticize leaders and make excuses when a job isn't done properly.

Therefore, you have to keep them on course, because the Bible says they're going to wander. Working with others really begins to get tough when you have told people what to do, and now have to say, "You're not doing it right." Clear instructions and a person's agreement to your instructions won't make him do it. That's your job. There's no substitute for someone standing by making sure it goes the way it's supposed to go.

Of course, the longer an individual has been with you, the more you'll know how tight or loose the supervision must be. Some people may require a daily check, others a monthly one. But supervision, of whatever frequency is a must.

When things are clearly not working and when people are not measuring up to your expectations, you have to find out root causes and determine what can be done. You know the tendency to stray is universal, but you must discover the practical reasons why it is occurring in this particular task at this particular time.

There are several basic causes (and many combinations of them) that an assignment is not performed to your satisfaction.

Personal Considerations

Often, a person's unsatisfactory performance may be due to personal factors we have overlooked. The problem is not primarily his but ours—shortsightedness. Consider the following possibilities:

1. Vague instructions—he has an unclear picture of what is expected of him.

2. He has encountered some problem which he may not yet fully recognize or about which he is slow to ask for help.

3. His goals have grown fuzzy. The standards of acceptable performance have not been made clear.

4. Training has been inadequate.

5. The job's importance has not been adequately stressed.

6. He is dependent on someone else or upon the completion of another piece of work which is slowing up his schedule.

7. He has personal problems on his mind—family, finances, illness, frustration, depression.

8. He has been placed in a position for which his temperament or personality is ill-suited.

9. This job is not compatible with his abilities.

10. He has not been challenged or properly motivated. We have failed to delegate and bring him into greater areas of responsiblity.

11. He has not been adequately praised and rewarded for past good performance.

12. His work has not been supervised regularly. Deviations from the standards have crept in without our or his being aware of it.

13. We have grown preoccupied with the results and have failed to view him as a total person. We haven't considered the personal and human requirements of his job. Evaluation has been too sterile, concerned with results alone.

14. He has a long history of good performance and we are now misjudging him on the basis of one poor evaluation.

15. The job is too big for him. He needs some help.

16. We have failed to involve him in the process of goal-setting to make his job more meaningful. We never ask his opinion or listen to him. We always just *tell* him what to do.

Almost always, when performance is sub-par, we can discover some of the reasons from this list.

Most people do not arrive at work every morning thinking up ways to shirk their responsibilities and make life miserable for their superiors. Most people, even if they are lazy, want to do a good job. Before cracking down heavily on poor performance, therefore, we must first check *ourselves*. Could poor performance be a result of our ineffectiveness as the leader?

The Path of Least Resistance

If you have taken all the proper managerial precautions—the person is suited to his job, is not suffering from personal difficulties, is capable of handling his responsibilities, has been trained and has shown in the past that he can do it—and yet performance remains below normal, then it is time to look to the man himself, at both his attitude and performance, and consider corrective measures to right the situation.

If you swing a pendulum or roll a ball down a hill, where does it stop? At the bottom of course. That's gravity.

Well there's a built-in gravitational pull within humans too. We tend to behave in the same way. We tend to stop at the bottom. When confronted with a choice we will usually choose the path of least resistance, the easy way out. That's another way of saying we're lazy.

When this tendency infects the work of your people, supervision becomes all the more vital. They will slow down and do things the easy, relaxed way. It occurs in many circumstances each day. When the alarm rings, it's easier to lie in bed than to get up. It's easier to sit with the TV on than to get up and turn it off. It's easier to stay inside by the fire than to suit up and run five miles in the rain. If we're told to dig a ditch 18 inches deep, it's easier to stop at 16, figuring, 'What's the difference? Who'll ever know?" If we're preparing a Bible study, it's easier to put it off until the night before than to get it out of the way the day after the assignment is given. If we're closing up the shop at 5:30 and the boss asks us to stay until 5:45 to take any late phone calls, it's the easy way out to leave at 5:40. It's easier for a woman to begin cooking dinner at 4:30 rather than tackling it at 11 in the morning. When you're tired and the children are misbehaving, it's easier to ignore them than to spend fifteen minutes in discipline and correction.

What we're dealing with here is laziness. What is needed is not ruthless discipline, but perhaps a tighter supervision. People frequently have to be reminded to get in gear. Even conscientious, dedicated people, unknowingly suffer from the path-of-least-resistance syndrome. As leader, your job is to keep the work pendulum from grinding to a halt. You have to give it an occasional shove.

Suppose that after exhausting all other possibilities, your supervision just doesn't seem to be working. There appears to be something willful, in addition to laziness, at work. Despite all your efforts, there remains a block in a person's attitude to complying with your requests. At this point you may begin to suspect another, and far more serious, root cause of poor performance—rebellion. At this point, discipline may be required.

Rebellion

In a business relationship there come times when a person is not doing his job simply because of willful rebellion. We are back once again to the nature of human nature. The Bible is clear that we all choose to be rebels at heart. My employee doesn't want to do what I asked, simply because he *wants* to go his own way. It has nothing to do with laziness. He just won't obey. It doesn't matter that I'm the boss and that he and I came to an agreement about his job. He doesn't want to do it.

It's hard to submit to another's leadership. It's natural to want to be free. Nevertheless, I have an important job to get done. Therefore, as a man's manager, if he and I agreed about a set of responsibilities, I must hold him to them. That's *my* responsibility. As a leader I have to deal with people who aren't complying with the program.

Modern theorists talk around this issue and want to work out every problem, according to some psychological tenet of interpersonal relationships. But when you're dealing with refusal to do a job you have to call it by its biblical name—*rebellion*. And rebellion is *sin*. A manager's personality does not cause a subordinate's rebellion. Selfishness does. If a man is asked to do something, and he resists, that is stubborn rebellion.

Now when *you* confront people and point out that they haven't been doing their jobs, don't expect them to jump up and down happily because you make them stay in line and point out the flaws in their performance. Human nature has another side which surfaced when Jesus was talking to a Pharisee who was "seeking to *justify* himself" (Luke 10:29). The moment you confront a person about what he didn't do, you can expect excuses.

Accepting full responsibility for failure is *very* difficult. It takes great humility. It's natural to try to cover up what we have done and pass responsibility elsewhere. And the smarter the person the more clever will be his excuse. Therefore, expect people to not only do things their own way, expect them to also justify themselves when confronted. Very rarely will someone say, "I made a mistake. I did not follow my instruction." That takes a higher degree of maturity than most have. Listen to your *own* words when *you* make a mistake. Don't you immediately list reasons why it is different in *this* particular case? why it was perfectly reasonable in light of *this* extenuating circumstance over which you had no control? There *are* justifiable explanations sometimes, but it is a human tendency to automatically revert to excuses.

When the Mark Is Missed

One of the most difficult things for a person responsible for the performance of others is to specifically pinpoint a problem and deal with it. Psychologist Henry Brandt has said, "The essence of management is to get there." We are often reluctant to determine whether we got there or not, and to affix responsibility if we fell short.

You have the difficult task of determining whether a person is sincerely trying, or if he is rebelling. If he is repentant, you are responsible to forgive.

You may still have to confront his failure to perform, but you can do so kindly. You don't have to get angry to tell him his job is unacceptable. Neither do you have to soft-pedal your words. You have to be *definite* when discussing shortcomings if you hope to get your point across.

You mustn't worry whether you're going to make someone happy or sad by what you say. Just make certain your attitude is right and your spirit friendly. You are not responsible for his joy. A person's joy must come from the Lord. His fulfillment in life is determined by his responses to God, not by his superior on the job. If he is a responsible person, he will *want* to be confronted with his liabilities because he wants to do a good job. You are responsible to help him do a better job—in positive, but honest, ways.

When you must move in with correction, mild measures should be tried before stringent ones. A minor problem often grows because it is not dealt with promptly. The sooner you act, the less likely you will need to use rigorous discipline later. If you abdicate this aspect of supervision, poor performance will multiply. Fair, firm correction will solve most problems by catching them early.

You need to determine motives and attitudes as you evaluate a person's potential future contribution. A person's attitude may be good, but there are times, despite all other factors involved, when an individual is just not going to work out. This is the vital aspect of evaluation—pinpointing the problems and deciding on solutions.

What do you do when an individual isn't reaching the mark and is showing *no* signs of change? When you recognize that you can no longer use that individual, that he is not contributing to your overall purpose, or that he is determined to go his own way in spite of clear-cut assignments, then you must remove him. Your job before God is to reach the goal, keeping your group on target toward what God has called you to do.

You must know your objectives clearly. You must weigh *all* potential explanations for poor performance, including your own managerial shortcomings. Try to devise solutions short of having to let him go, enabling you to minister to his deep needs. Do everything possible to be lenient, but not at the expense of what God has given you to do. When the worker is not contributing to that team effort, you have no option. You must prune the vine.

The Israelites—A Straying People

The Israelites had as godly a man to lead them as one could imagine. And though they time and again witnessed the hand of God delivering them, they continued to go their own way. They would not consistently follow either Moses or the Lord. Their forty years in the desert were spent oscillating between obedience and disobedience.

The peoples' mistrust and complaining spread to Moses' own family. Aaron and Miriam spoke against him. When Moses was on the mountain, who was it that led the people astray? It was Aaron, his top man, the second in command. Even Moses slipped at Meribah. People tend to go their own way, even as high up as Aaron and Moses.

If you think following leadership principles changes this, examine the Israelites further. If you want to see thorough standards, study the books of Exodus and Leviticus. God left *nothing* to chance—"Fold the sixth curtain double at the front of the tent. Make fifty loops along the edge of the end" (Ex. 26:9-10, NIV). What a demonstration of precision and order!

God's requirements for obedience were perfect and clear. And the Israelites promised, "We will do as the Lord commands!" Yet is it surprising they failed to follow through on their commitment?

No matter how much you do right as a leader, your people will not always follow through on their commitments. You may even find, as Moses did, that your most trusted man builds a golden calf.

All the people strayed. Even Moses. Some (such as Aaron) were retrievable; others (such as Dathan) were not. You, as a leader, will have to differentiate between these two types of workers.

Even you the leader, must learn your own limits, for you too, are susceptible to the nature of human nature.

Evaluate Yourself

1. Am I able to courageously, yet compassionately, evaluate my people? Where is supervision lacking? Which people require a tighter rein?
2. Which of the following is the key factor in each of my "problem people"?
   a. Personal considerations.
   b. The path of least resistance.
   c. Rebellion.
3. What measures should I take to help each of these people?

13. A PROBLEM-ORIENTED MENTALITY

Positive and Negative—Keep a Balance

As an observant person you must keep an eye peeled for trouble. You must develop a problem-oriented mentality.

This does not imply pessimism. It simply means that despite your optimism about what you have to do, you need to isolate those aspects that need help. Like the carnivorous cat which has an instinct for the jugular, you must develop an instinct for problems. Even while supplying inspiration you ask, "What improvements can we make? What's the weak link? What's not working well?"

You will constantly walk a tightrope—between reaching a goal and developing people; between ordering, "Get with it!" (as Moses did in Exodus 32:26), and exercising great patience. The spiritual leader cannot allow his attitudes to be governed by pat formulas. As he or she daily maintains this balance, he must exercise a positive outlook undergirded by a loving spirit.

Expect Success

Exercising patience does not imply we excuse someone when he misses the mark he's supposed to hit. Saying, "It's okay, it doesn't matter that it isn't *quite* right" (except in justified cases) signals weakness of purpose. For if you've carefully drawn up a detailed plan for reaching certain goals, then it *does* matter. When you have a blueprint, every part depends on every other part. The moment you start saying one thing doesn't have to measure up to the standard, the whole thing begins to get sloppy and fall apart.

I depend heavily on information from my store managers arriving on my desk by certain days of each month. I need inventory figures by the 2nd, sales figures by the 3rd, expenses by the 6th, and invoices by the 8th. I have a monthly checklist of over 25 separate items of paperwork I must take care of. Every item is important. Each hinges on my receiving certain key information from our other stores, information which must arrive on time and in a format I have prescribed. If it's late, my work will be late. If it's incomplete, I must finish someone else's work before I can get to my own.

It *does* matter that a job's done right. Certainly there's flexibility—when a man is new to a particular assignment, it will take him possibly several months to learn the routine. And it's normal that occasional mistakes creep in. But when an individual consistently does not comply with the instructions and is late month-after-month, he throws the entire accounting process off. We then run the risk of penalties for late tax filings, and the bookkeeping bogs down and spills over into the following month. Getting it right *does* matter.

Do I simply shrug it off each time and say, "It's okay. You're doing a great job otherwise. We'll manage even if we are a little late."

No. It isn't a question of the work being just a *little* bit off. I have given certain instructions. There has been a training period. Everyone understands the assignment and if it falls within the range of capability.

Therefore I expect it to be *done*. That doesn't make me an insensitive, authoritarian manager. It simply means I have deadlines to meet. I don't want our business in trouble with the government for missing those deadlines. So when I say, "Make sure I have sales figures by the 3rd," I expect them by the 3rd.

You must operate in an atmosphere where success is the norm. You must expect things to be done right. You must strive for perfection in the carrying out of normal instructions. You do not expect people themselves to be perfect, but you have structured your expectations to take the human element into account. Therefore, once you activate your plan you expect it to be carried out perfectly, unless some major factor makes that impossible.

Your responsibility is to reach your objectives by carrying out your plan—*all* of it. You can't construct a house properly by omitting a 2 x 4 here, a piece of plywood there, and a length of wiring someplace else. You must comply with *everything* on your blueprint and carry it out 100 percent. Leaders, like builders, must isolate and remove *anything* that hinders the successful following of the blueprints. While you "expect" success, you recognize there will be diversions. When that happens, your job is to get things back where they belong as soon as possible so you can continue on.

This involves an assumption about each of your people. If you have trained someone and worked with him, if you have done your job, he is prepared and qualified to do as instructed—perfectly. He is not expected to *be* perfect. But he does have the skill and experience to do the job right.

You are, therefore, springing no surprises when you hold him to that job—all of it. This has nothing to do with being strict. For example, God told the Israelites, "You shall have no other gods before me" (Ex. 20:3). When Moses was on the mountain they only made one other god, just one golden calf. How strict was God going to be? After all, it was just *one*—they didn't really miss the mark by much.

But the instructions had been precise—*no other gods.* And the people had agreed to follow the instructions: "We will do everything the Lord has said" (19:8). Therefore, God's reply to Moses was clear: "Whoever has sinned against me, I will blot out of my book. Now go, lead the people" (32:33).

When I talk to one of my co-workers about a persisting problem, I'm not interested in all sorts of explanations about why the job hasn't been done time after time. The people who work for me are professionals and I treat them as such. Many aspects of our store operation, from mail processing to expense percentages, have clear-cut standards. They are not optional. They determine how the stores function. No one comes to work for me unless he has read the manual and says, "I'm willing to work under these conditions, with such expectations on me."

Therefore, they cannot later rationalize, "I was one percent over the advertising budget and two percent over the salary budget for the Christmas season. But the local TV station was having a special on 30-second spots, and I felt we needed some extra part-time help in the store, and. . . ."

At that point I'm not as concerned with *why* it happened as with whether the budget is going to be where it belongs next month. If we miss the mark by "just a little" in several key areas, our scant profit margin of three to five percent is quickly gone and we are in the red.

You *must* set standards because they are important. You *must* reach them. If the goals don't need to be reached, don't bother setting them. If they are too high and your people are straining under the pressure, then modify them. But you mustn't set important, meaningful goals and then act as if nothing had happened if they are missed.

Finding the Squeak

I'm sure you've had the experience of driving along past pleasant scenery, in brilliant sunshine. But your car develops an annoying squeak. The scenery becomes irrelevant. Before long the squeak is driving you crazy and you know you've got to isolate it and give it a shot of WD-40.

If you are going to be productive and get more done, you

must deal with the squeaks, with the one percent of things that aren't quite up to par, with the things that, to the outside observer, can appear minor. To the passerby, the problem-conscious leader sometimes looks like an IRS auditor, determinedly sniffing around to find something amiss. Everything appears to be flowing smoothly enough on the surface so what difference could a few inefficiencies make anyhow?

But the activities of an astute leader are far more than nit-picking. He knows his plan inside out. He has watched it grow. He knows those crucial points where the stress is focused. He knows what is important to the continued smooth working of all the parts. He noses around because he knows it is essential that squeaks be caught immediately rather than be allowed to develop into major problems.

Pinpoint problems as soon as they begin. You ought to find yourself drawn to problems. Not because you hope to rid your operation of every one (that will never happen!), but so you can nip them in the bud.

To keep from irritating your people with your critical analysis, you must maintain a positive atmosphere of friendliness, goodwill, and mutual respect. Your people must know that you appreciate them, are pulling for them, and are glad to be working with them. They must sense your confidence in them. A spirit of camaraderie and thankfulness must flow from you.

Only when this spirit of positive relationships exists will you be able to deal with problems without alienating people.

Many assume people will pick up such appreciation automatically, by osmosis. ("He knows I appreciate his work. I don't have to praise him for it."). This is not true. People need *verbal* praise. Once such an upbeat atmosphere is established, you can, as the need arises, deal straightforwardly with troubles.

If your relationships are positive, you don't have to take

pains to create a positive atmosphere each time you sit down to discuss a problem. If you have done your prior job well, you can take the positiveness for granted. You know your people are skilled and capable and they know you know. For you have communicated confidence. Mutual respect is constantly reinforced.

But your task is to discover and remove anything that hinders 100 percent success. You will help someone become even *more* successful because you are going to point out flaws he is unable to see. The dedicated person will *want* to see you come and will *want* to hear your criticism. He *wants* to improve and he knows your experience and perspective will help him uncover those areas where he needs work. He knows your criticism is motivated out of genuine concern.

Finding the squeaks isn't negative. It's entirely *positive*. The proper attitude is, "Wow! If we do this, things will get even *better*!" rather than, "You did this wrong!" Uncover flaws *positively*.

When my college track coach approached me during a work-out, it usually was not to say, "You ran a great race last weekend." If I had run a good race we both knew it. Success was the whole idea. We both expected me to run good races. That was, in a sense, my job description, the whole purpose of my being on the track team.

My coach and I had a relationship of respect that had developed through the years. I knew he appreciated me and I didn't expect a compliment every time he saw me. Therefore, when he came over to me during practice, it was usually to isolate and deal with a problem—"Come off that turn at 7/8 speed. I want to look at the way your foot meets the track. Something doesn't look quite right."

I was always glad when I saw him coming. It was my opportunity to improve my running because his critical eye watched everything I did and pointed out my flaws. I was particularly hungry for his criticism after I had run a *bad* race. His knowledge and experience made him much more capable of assessing my needs than I was. I wanted to be a better runner and I knew *he* knew more about it than I did. So I eagerly hung on his every word and then fervently practiced whatever he told me to do. Though his words were often critical, he forced me to confront those areas where I needed to make improvements. His were entirely positive contributions, ones I appreciated, because I knew he believed in me.

The same type of relationship exists between myself and my store managers. When I go into one of our stores, I don't have to go through a half hour of preliminaries, telling the manager what a great job he's doing. I have taken care of that earlier. Throughout the weeks and months as we correspond and talk on the phone, I have expressed appreciation and confidence. We have a relationship which is founded on a mutal respect.

But if I'm in the store to talk about some problems, neither of us has time to beat around the bush. In the short time we have together, I want to find and deal with the flaws, those areas that aren't going as well as they might. If his heart is right toward his job and toward me, he is glad to see me coming. He knows I am on his side, so we can get down to business.

My job is that of trouble-shooter, squeak-finder, problem-solver. When I come into a store, I usually find everything running at 99 percent efficiency. Employees are at the counter, someone is being shown a Bible at the Bible display, the cash register is ringing, the customers are enjoying the music, the stock on the shelves looks good.

So what do I have to say?

"There are some dead leaves on the plant over there. The window display is looking a little shoddy. There's a girl working in the mail room while customers are stacking up at the counter; remind her to wait on customers first."

That's my function—to bring the problems to someone's attention. I don't have to review the 99 percent every time. I get right to the squeaks—"Pick up the leaves, change the window display, and remind your people that the counter comes before the mail room." I can do this because I've previously dealt with these areas in the manual.

Why Must We Be So Negative?

You may be asking, "All this emphasis on the problems—can't we just focus on the goals, remain positive, and trust God to remove the obstacles that come up? This 'problem-oriented mentality' you're talking about could get me down and sap my enthusiasm."

That attitude will work fine if your goals aren't clear and if there's nothing specific you feel you *must* do. In such a case, if you're moving in one direction and you encounter a tree across the path, what's to stop you from simply changing direction? That's fine if it doesn't really matter where you go.

But if you are *determined* to get where you want to go, then it matters a great deal that you get over, under, or around that tree, for you *must* continue on the same path. Therefore you can't ignore the obstacles.

If you want to build a house, or lead your study group through the book of Job, or write a book, you must be aware of and deal with things that stand in your way. If you suddenly discover an underground spring under your building site, or if some contentious man in your group insists on pointlessly sidetracking your discussion, or if your typewriter conks out, what will you do?

That is the point. How well prepared are you to deal with the unexpected trees that fall across your path? If you're going to get to where you're going and reach your goals, you must continue on the path to the end.

Evaluate Yourself

1. Do I maintain a positive/negative balance in my person-

ality? Does the "1 percent-squeak mentality" make me unusually negative?

2. Do I easily communicate appreciation and success? Have I established a climate of goodwill among my people?

3. Am I able to convey optimism, even when dealing with difficulties?

14. START GETTING MORE DONE!

We began this book with a discussion of time and how to use it more effectively. We saw the critical role of self-discipline and decision-making in the use of our time. We talked about productivity and accomplishment, about achieving the goals the Lord puts in our hearts. We discovered that *it is possible to do just about anything we choose to do.* Seeing this happen in *your* life or mine depends on the goals we set, the plans we devise, and what we do with them.

We then turned our attention to what it takes to work effectively with people as we progress toward our goals. We looked at leadership principles that can enable us to work with others to reach our objectives. We examined the need to be aware of problems and to be able to deal with them.

Where do you go from here?

Quite simply, *you* are at a crossroads in your life. As you now stand and look out into the future, you really can do anything or become anything you want—if you follow these principles. It won't be easy and it won't happen tomorrow, but *it can happen!*

It's up to you to choose. You can place this book on a shelf to collect dust and never think of it again; and your life will progress just as it has for years.

Or you can, like Dave Jenkins, say to yourself, "Hey, I *can* do it. I'm going to achieve my goals!"

You can visualize what you want to do and be, and then set out to achieve it. And you *can* reach it!

If you are determined to launch out and exercise dominion over what God has in store for you, I encourage you,

155

with your goal or goals firmly in mind, to begin re-reading this book tomorrow. Read from the perspective of *knowing* that you *are* going to *achieve* something significant. Read through it slowly, confidently, taking all the time you need on the evaluation questions. Formulate the step-by-step plan that will take you from where you are right now—today—to where you want to be in the future. Use pencil and paper and *write*. Make this second time through a working session. Don't try to read and write your ideas while you're lying in bed drifting off to sleep.

Believe me, if you follow this procedure (and especially if you follow the advice in Chapter 7—perhaps the most important chapter of all!), you'll never be the same again. In a few months (even weeks), you won't recognize your life. It's up to you. If you want to, you *can* do it!

WORKSHEET #1 — *Maintaining a Rigorous Routine*

Which of your regular activities could benefit by being done at the same time every day, week, or month?

Activity	Frequency	Usual Time
Get up	Daily	
Quiet time—pray, read, plan, etc.	Daily	
Go to bed	Daily	

Using the following form, construct a schedule for your regular activities. You may want to make copies of this page and experiment with various schedules.

	Morning			Afternoon		Evening
	-8	8-10	10-12	12-3	3-6	6-
Sunday						
Monday						
Tuesday						
Wednesday						
Thursday						
Friday						
Saturday						

WORKSHEET #2 — *Formulating Major Objectives*

List on separate sheets of paper, the goals you have for various areas of your life. Make them clear and concise, for they will become the foundation as you proceed. Use a pencil so that you can make refinements. List them in this form. Be imaginative. Have courage to dream BIG DREAMS!!

Areas to Consider

Spiritual growth
Relationship with spouse
Children
Church life
Friends
Organizations
Bible study
Prayer life
Reading
Exercise and recreation
Hobbies
Finances
Education

Service to others
Career achievement
Home
Retirement
Creative projects
Travel
Community involvement
Social action
Secondary vocational
    pursuits
Odd jobs
Others

Area of Life _____

Long-Range Objective:

Intermediate Objectives:

Immediate Objectives:

Accomplishment depends on the ability to dream and to formulate specific goals from those dreams. Visualize successful achievements with yourself in the picture. Believe in your goals with expectancy. Such thoughts are self-fulfilling; they act as magnets to pull your actions in line. The brain will produce a reality in line with whatever you feed it.

WORKSHEET # 3 — *Planning for Simple Goals*

On scratch paper, list every activity necessary to attain a certain goal. Then prioritize with A's, B's, and C's or 1's, 2's, and 3's to formulate an orderly progression. Write, rewrite, erase, try again. It's impossible to write a really good plan on the first attempt.

Exact steps necessary to reach this goal:	Contingencies: information needed, people involved:	Completion schedule— deadlines:	Resources needed:

Concise statement of final objective: Final deadline:

WORKSHEET # 4 — *Planning for Complex Goals*

Exact steps necessary to reach this goal:	Contingencies: information needed, people involved:	Deadlines for the the start and finish of each activity:	Resources needed:
Immediate Activities			
Checkpoint:			
Intermediate Activities			
Checkpoint:			
Checkpoint:			
Concise statement of final objective—		Final deadline:	

Some plans will be so complicated you will need to draw up complete sub-plans for certain aspects. Don't be bound by these planning forms. Modify them into whatever format helps you get where you want to go. *Follow your plan!*